Contents

Unit 5: Ratio Analysis

Unit 6: Financial Information in the Media – Company Shares and Bonds

Unit 7: Financial Information in the Media – and Financial Trading

UNDERSTANDING BUSINESS

FINANCIAL INFORMATION

MADE EASY

Rob Dransfield

Published in 2002 by:
Nelson Thornes Ltd
Delta Place
27 Bath Road
CHELTENHAM
GL53 7TH
United Kingdom

A catalogue record for this book is available from the British
Library

ISBN 0 7487 6679 0

01 02 03 04 05 / 10 9 8 7 6 5 4 3 2 1

Diagrams by GreenGate Publishing Services and Derek Griffin,
cartoons by Nathan Betts

Page make-up by GreenGate Publishing Services, Tonbridge, Kent

Printed and bound in Great Britain by Scotprint

The author would like to thank Jane Gilby and Sandy Marshall at
Nelson Thornes, and GreenGate Publishing Services for their help
in the preparation of this book.

Thanks are due to the following for permission to use material
reproduced in this book:

Boots p.6 and p.22, Domino's Pizza UK & IRL plc p.22, Halifax p.6,
lastminute.com p.6, London Stock Exchange p.10, Marks and
Spencer p.6, PA photos p.63, The Tytherington Club,
www.clubhaus.com p.50, W I Link plc p.95.

Introduction

This book has been written to help you to develop quickly a good understanding of the main types of financial information that you will come across in the financial sections of national newspapers and in company reports.

To many people, financial information appears to be difficult to penetrate because of the sheer volume of such information and the seemingly impenetrable way that it is presented. For example, the majority of the population will skip over the financial sections of a quality newspaper because they have never had finance explained to them.

This book therefore seeks to provide you with a systematic and structured guide to financial information and reporting, showing you that these subjects are a lot easier to understand than they at first appear. However, we have not sought to oversimplify because you need to be able to use financial information in the way that it is presented to you. The book draws on a number of recent extracts of information taken from company reports of well known companies.

Doctor Proctor is our vehicle for helping and guiding you through the key features of financial information, including financial reporting. We hope you find him to be a helpful and sympathetic guide.

About the author

Rob Dransfield is a Senior Lecturer in Business, Economics and Quantitative Methods at the Nottingham Trent University. He has also worked at the University of Mauritius, MIE, as an external examiner for accounts.

How to Use this Book

As you work through the text, you'll find the following features to help you.

Key Ideas

These are some of the fundamental ideas on which finance and accounting is based.

Key Ideas ⊙⟶

Components of a profit and loss account

You Must Know This

Terms and principles that you need to learn by heart and understand.

Dr Proctor says:
'You Must Know This!'

Financial reports are documents which communicate information about the financial position and performance of an organisation to interested parties.

Doctor Proctor Calculates

Learn these methods of calculation – you'll save yourself a lot of time!

Doctor Proctor Calculates

$$\text{Gearing ratio} = \frac{\text{Net debt + Preference shares}}{\text{Ordinary share capital}}$$

Distinguish Between...

Here you need to be able to explain the difference between one term or concept and another.

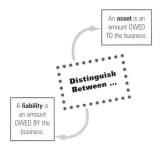

An **asset** is an amount OWED TO the business.

Distinguish Between ...

A **liability** is an amount OWED BY the business.

Doctor Proctor Outlines ...

Explanations of important themes and ideas in finance and accountancy.

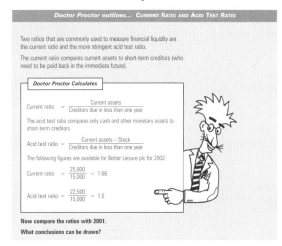

Doctor Proctor outlines... CURRENT RATIO AND ACID TEST RATIO

Two ratios that are commonly used to measure financial liquidity are the current ratio and the more stringent acid test ratio.

The current ratio compares current assets to short-term creditors (who need to be paid back in the immediate future).

Doctor Proctor Calculates

$$\text{Current ratio} = \frac{\text{Current assets}}{\text{Creditors due in less than one year}}$$

The acid test ratio compares only cash and other monetary assets to short-term creditors.

$$\text{Acid test ratio} = \frac{\text{Current assets} - \text{Stock}}{\text{Creditors due in less than one year}}$$

The following figures are available for Better Leisure plc for 2002:

$$\text{Current ratio} = \frac{25,000}{15,000} = 1.66$$

$$\text{Acid test ratio} = \frac{22,500}{15,000} = 1.5$$

Now compare the ratios with 2001.
What conclusions can be drawn?

Activities

Practical accounting problems for you to puzzle out.

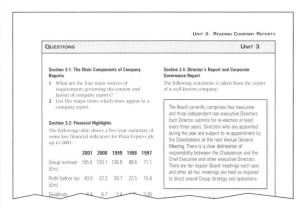

Activity

Which of these two companies had the higher profit margin in 2000?

	Fitness First plc	Holmes Place plc
	£000	£000
Turnover	52,234	87,699
Operating profit	13,036	15,896

Questions and Answers

Short, practical exercises to test your understanding.

UNIT 3: READING COMPANY REPORTS

QUESTIONS **UNIT 3**

Section 3.1: The Main Components of Company Reports
1 What are the four main sources of requirements governing the content and layout of company reports?
2 List five major items which must appear in a company report.

Section 3.2: Financial Highlights
The following table shows a five-year summary of some key financial indicators for Pizza Express plc up to 2001.

	2001	2000	1999	1998	1997
Group turnover (£m)	185.6	150.1	126.6	99.6	71.1
Profit before tax (£m)	40.0	32.2	28.7	22.5	15.6
Dividends	8.4	6.7	5.4		3.35

Section 3.4: Director's Report and Corporate Governance Report
The following statement is taken from the report of a well known company:

The Board currently comprises four executive and three independent non-executive Directors. Each Director submits for re-election at least every three years. Directors who are appointed during the year are subject to re-appointment by the Shareholders at the next Annual General Meeting. There is a clear delineation of responsibility between the Chairperson and the Chief Executive and other executive Directors. There are ten regular Board meetings each year and other ad hoc meetings are held as required to direct overall Group strategy and operations.

UNIT 1
INTRODUCTION

Topics covered in this unit

1.1 Sources of Financial Information

A description of the major types of financial information, ranging from company reports to the financial press.

1.2 The Main Users of Financial Reports

Shows that it is not just investors that read financial reports but a range of other groups including employees, financial journalists, suppliers, lenders of funds, etc.

This unit explains why it is so important to understand financial information, including the information presented in financial reports. It also describes the main users of financial reports and financial information and the use they make of this information.

1.1 SOURCES OF FINANCIAL INFORMATION

Key Ideas

Financial reporting

Financial reports provide information in numbers, words and pictures about the financial performance of organisations.

Doctor Proctor outlines... THE IMPORTANCE OF BEING ABLE TO INTERPRET FINANCIAL INFORMATION

Everybody needs to know something about financial information and financial reporting because although you may not own any stocks and shares you and your friends and family may work for an organisation. To gain more details about how these organisations are faring you will need to be able to read and interpret financial information. In addition, many people have money invested in a pension fund, belong to a trade union, or have savings in a financial institution. These bodies invest the money that you pay into them in financial securities. If they invest wisely you are safe and will do well, if they invest poorly you may find that your hard-earned savings are frittered away. In addition, many researchers (including students carrying out a research project) need to carry out in-depth studies of company reports. These researchers need to understand what company information means and the various ways in which it is presented.

Every day vast quantities of financial information are produced. Some appears in company reports, government reports and the reports of other organisations such as schools and hospitals. Financial information is also produced about prices and trading on the various financial and commodity markets including the money markets (markets for short-term funds), capital markets (markets for long-term funds such as the Stock Exchange), and commodity markets (such as metal and grain exchanges).

In addition, newspapers and magazines provide reams of financial information for both the specialist and the non-specialist. And of course, the Internet has become a major source of financial information because as a medium it is able to provide up-to-the-minute information.

This book is therefore concerned with outlining:

*   the users of financial reports and financial information;

*   the nature and purpose of financial reports; and

*   the interpretation of financial information.

Dr Proctor says:
'You Must Know This!'

Financial reports are documents which communicate information about the financial position and performance of an organisation to interested parties.

1.2 THE MAIN USERS OF FINANCIAL REPORTS

Key Ideas

Users of financial reports

There are a number of groups who will want to use financial reports to meet their information needs. These are the same groups who will use the financial press and the Internet to gain more financial information.

Investors

Investors are private individuals and financial institutions (e.g. insurance companies, pension funds, etc.) that buy shares in a company. As shareholders they become part owners of companies. Investors buy shares in the hope of making a return on the shares, either in the form of good dividends (their share of the profit) and/or because the shares increase in value.

In this country shareholders are the main users of company reports and therefore many of the laws and requirements relating to company reports are made with shareholders in mind.

Employees

Employees and trade unions read company reports to find out how secure employment is in their company. They are also interested in the profitability of the company because this can inform wage demands for the coming year. Many employees also own shares in their company.

Lenders

Banks and other lenders study company reports to check that the company is able to pay the interest on money lent and eventually to pay the sum that they have loaned.

Suppliers and other creditors

Businesses that have supplied a company with goods on credit, and other creditors will want to be sure that they will be paid on time. Before offering credit to a company, it therefore makes sense to study their financial reports.

Customers

Regular customers of a company will want to check that it will be capable of supplying them well into the future. Studying the financial report gives them a good picture of how healthy the business is that they are dealing with.

Government

Government statistical departments collect information about business results taken across the country. Specialist government agencies such as the Inland Revenue will need to study reports to assess tax liabilities for corporation tax, for example, which is the tax on profits.

The public

The wider public uses financial reports for a number of reasons; for example, business students will use reports for study purposes, while people in a local community may want to examine the impact of changes in the company or the local environment on jobs.

Journalists

Financial and business journalists use business reports to find out about the health of the economy as a whole, the health of different sectors of the economy, and the health of individual businesses. The reports of financial journalists are read widely and used by the other users of financial information outlined above.

Topics covered in this unit

The most important type of financial information is about companies and their performance. This unit explains what a company is, how companies are set up, and how companies secure long-term finance through the Stock Exchange.

2.1 What is a Company?
Describes the main types of private sector business and shows how private (Ltd) and public companies fit into this pattern.

2.2 Controlling the Activities of Companies
Shows how companies are registered, and the documents that need to be created, which govern relationships within the company and relationships with the outside world.

2.3 The Role of Directors
Sets out the roles and responsibilities of directors of companies and shows their relationship with investors.

2.4 The Role of the Stock Exchange
Explains how the Stock Exchange provides a market for company securities, and supports companies in the acquisition of long-term capital.

2.5 Unit Trusts
Shows how unit trusts enable investors to spread their risks while providing capital for business activity.

2.6 Investment Trusts
Explains how investment trusts provide long-term capital for business and also provide investors with a steady return, depending on how much risk they are willing to take.

2.7 Types of Shares
Companies are owned by shareholders. There are two main types of shareholder – preference and ordinary shareholders.

2.8 Sources of Third Party Finance
Describes the main types of external finance available to a company.

Questions

2.1 WHAT IS A COMPANY?

Key Ideas

Joint stock company

The owners (shareholders) jointly put a stock of capital (money) into the business. They then are entitled to a share of the profits in the form of a dividend.

Everyone is familiar with some of this country's largest companies and their activities. Obvious examples are Richard Branson's Virgin, which is involved in rail and air transport, and which produces Virgin Cola and Mates contraceptives; BP, which is a major oil and gas company, and Cadbury-Schweppes, which produces chocolate, confectionery and soft drinks. However, not everyone knows how a company is set up, and the legal status of companies.

An Act of Parliament of 1844 recognised all joint stock companies that registered under it as bodies in their own right. The joint stock company thus became a body which was separate from the individuals who owned that company.

Dr Proctor says:

'You Must Know This!'

A company is a group of people who share responsibility for a business venture.

Doctor Proctor outlines... TYPES OF BUSINESS

There are four main types of private business in the UK:

1 **A sole trader.** This is the business consisting of one person that is typically associated with window cleaners, plumbers, electricians and one-person-owned shops.

2 **A partnership.** This involves two or more partners and is set up by registering a deed of partnership with a solicitor. Partnerships are associated with vets, doctors, dentists, solicitors, corner shops and other small businesses where people share skills, and the profits.

Neither the sole trader nor the ordinary partnership has limited liability.

3 **Private companies.** These are registered private companies with at least two shareholders. The shareholders appoint a Board of Directors. Shares in the company are sold privately with the permission of the Board of Directors. Typically private companies are small and medium-sized companies. Shareholders have the protection of limited liability.

4 **Public companies.** These are companies whose shares are traded on the Stock Exchange. They are usually large companies and all shareholders are protected by limited liability. Well-known examples of public limited companies include Marks & Spencer, Cadbury-Schweppes, Boots, Halifax, LastMinute.Com, etc.

MARKS & SPENCER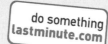

2.1 WHAT IS A COMPANY?

Limited liability

Shareholders in a company are given a very important legal protection known as limited liability. Limited liability means that should a company run into financial difficulties and run up debts, the maximum amount that the shareholders are liable to pay of this debt is the value of their shareholding. This means that although the shareholders are part owners of the company they will not be expected to sell off their personal possessions and property to pay the debts of the company.

Other types of business

Other types of business in this country are:

Franchises: A **franchisor** can sell a **franchise** (right to trade under a well-known name in a particular area) to a **franchisee**. This arrangement is growing in popularity and is common in the fast-food sector, in plumbing and cleaning services and in distribution, as well as many other areas.

Co-operatives: A co-operative is made up of a group of producers, sellers or workers working collaboratively in an enterprise.

Mutual societies: A mutual is an organisation which is set up and run to serve its members. Many building societies typically took this form – although today many are converting to plc status in order to be able to raise more capital.

In this book we are mainly concerned with the activities of private and public companies.

Example

The growth of Marks and Spencer

Marks and Spencer provides a good example of a business that went through these four stages. Initially Michael Marks started out as a sole trader, hawking items such as needles and thread from door to door. He was a Jewish immigrant from Russia who arrived in England in the late nineteenth century, speaking little English.

He formed a business partnership with Tom Spencer, and they opened up a number of market stalls in the North of England. Tom Spencer only stayed in the business for a short period of time.

The business then expanded by becoming a private company, with shares largely being held in the

Marks and Sieff families (two families connected by marriage). Excited by new mass retailing methods in America the families decided to open up a chain of shops – giving rise to the M&S that we know today. Again, more finance was required to fund the expansion – hence the need to become a public company.

2.2 CONTROLLING THE ACTIVITIES OF COMPANIES

Key Ideas

Registering for corporate status

The way in which businesses are set up and run in this country is controlled by a series of Companies Acts.

There are two types of limited joint stock companies:

1   **Private limited companies.** These have **Ltd** after their name. A limited company can not offer shares to the general public.

2   **Public limited companies.** These have **plc** after their name and they can issue shares to the general public, provided that they have more than £50,000 of capital.

Companies must register two documents with the **Registrar of Companies** before they can receive a **Certificate of Incorporation**, enabling them to become a corporate body recognised in law.

The **Memorandum** needs to cover the following:

*   The name of the company.
*   The address of the registered office.
*   The objectives of the company.
*   The face value of the capital invested in the business.
*   The amounts of different types of share capital.

If a company tries to carry out activities which go beyond the scope of its objectives then this might be held by a court of law to be *ultra vires* – beyond its powers and thus not allowable.

The **Articles** constitute a contract between the company and its shareholders. The names of the shareholders are kept on a company register of shareholders.

Articles include details of when shareholders' meetings will take place, the voting rights of shareholders, etc.

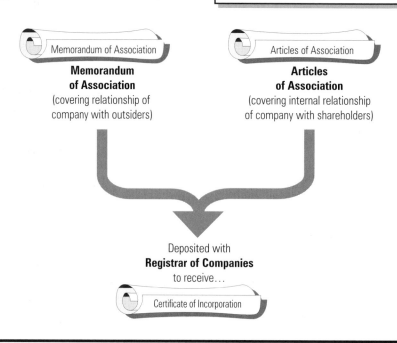

Memorandum of Association

Memorandum of Association
(covering relationship of company with outsiders)

Articles of Association

Articles of Association
(covering internal relationship of company with shareholders)

Deposited with
Registrar of Companies
to receive…

Certificate of Incorporation

2.3 THE ROLE OF DIRECTORS

Key Ideas 🔑

Corporate governance

Shareholders own a company. The company will have a number of assets (what it owns, and what it is owed) and liabilities (what it owes).

Dr Proctor says:
'You Must Know This!'

Corporate governance is the system by which companies are directed and controlled.

The shareholders appoint **directors** to run the company on their behalf. Executive directors are ones with a responsibility for putting decisions into practice. Non-executive directors are ones who provide advice to the Board and help the company through their contacts.

Directors are required to report each year about their stewardship of the company. Shareholders can attend the Annual General Meeting and ask questions about the running of the business. Shareholders can vote at the AGM. Their voting rights are often proportionate to the number of shares they hold.

Shareholders vote to accept the annual report presented by the directors, and they can vote on the re-appointment of members of the Board.

Directors can appoint managers to manage the company on their behalf. Most companies are required to have at least two directors.

A **Chair of the Board** chairs directors' meetings and the AGM. However, the chair is often different from the managing director, who plays a key role in the management of the organisation. (The Cadbury Committee on corporate governance recommended that the role of chair and managing director (chief executive) of a company should be separate, but this is not a legal requirement.)

The **Board of Directors** has a collective responsibility for the stewardship of the company.

Shareholders play a role in appointing and dismissing directors. However, the managing director plays a key role in appointing executive directors, i.e. ones who are responsible for carrying out decisions within the company.

The chair and non-executive directors can play an important part in removing the managing director by voting on the Board. However, in law directors can only be removed by shareholders.

We can illustrate the role of the Board of Directors by means of an example:

Example

Thistle Hotels owns and operates hotels in the UK, including many in London.

The Board consists of three executive and seven non-executive directors. Apart from the Chairman, the Deputy Chairman is the Senior Independent Non-Executive Director of the Company. Each director must retire by rotation at least every three years, under the Company's Articles of Association.

The Board meets regularly throughout the year to review the Company's financial and operational performance and to consider those matters formally reserved for the decision of the Board. These include strategy, acquisition and divestment policy, approval of budgets and major capital expenditure, and general treasury and risk management policies. Directors are provided with timely and appropriate information in advance of each Board meeting, regarding the trading and financial affairs of the Group.

2.4 THE ROLE OF THE STOCK EXCHANGE

Key Ideas

Stock Exchange

The main **advantage** of selling shares through the Stock Exchange is that large amounts of capital can be raised very quickly.

Two **disadvantages** are:

- control of a business can be lost by the original shareholders if large quantities of shares are purchased as part of a 'takeover bid';

- it is also costly to have shares quoted on the Stock Exchange.

Doctor Proctor outlines... THE STOCK EXCHANGE

The Stock Exchange is one of the most important institutions in British business because it provides a means through which investors can buy and sell shares in hundreds of different public limited companies. Investors know that they can buy shares on the Stock Exchange and just as importantly they can have their shares sold. The buying and selling of shares is carried out by intermediaries – brokers and market makers who make a profit from these transactions.

A public company has its shares bought and sold on the Stock Exchange. Companies can go to the expense of having a '**full quotation**' on the Stock Exchange, so their share prices appear on the dealers' visual display screens.

To create a public company, the directors must apply to the **Stock Exchange Council**, which will carefully check the accounts.

UK companies listed on the London Stock Exchange must meet the informational requirements set out in the 'Yellow Book', **Admissions of Securities to Listing**. This sets out how they must present their accounts. Listed companies must also produce a half-yearly or interim report.

The Stock Exchange requires all listed UK companies to state in their annual report whether they are complying with the Code of Best Practice on Corporate Governance. They must give reasons for any areas of non-compliance. This code of best practice was set up in 1992 by the Cadbury Committee, which set out to make sure that accounts are presented in a clear and fair way.

2.4 THE ROLE OF THE STOCK EXCHANGE

Doctor Proctor outlines... HOW COMPANIES CAN 'GO PUBLIC'

A business wanting to '**go public**' will arrange for a merchant bank to handle the paperwork. Selling new shares is quite a risky business. The Stock Exchange has 'good days' (when a great many people want to buy shares) and 'bad days' (when a great many people want to sell). If the issue of new shares coincides with a bad day (e.g. September 11th 2001), a company can find itself in difficulties.

Example

If the company hopes to sell a million new shares at 100 pence each and all goes well it will raise £1 million (1 million × £1); on a bad day, however, it might be able to sell only half its shares at this price. There is quite a lot of luck involved, therefore, in choosing the launch day of new shares because the date has to be chosen well in advance. Some companies are very unlucky, launching their shares on a day when people are gloomy about prospects in the economy.

One way around this problem is to arrange a 'placing' with a merchant bank. The merchant bank recommends the company's shares to some of the share-buying institutions with which it deals (pension funds and insurance companies, for example), who may then agree to buy a certain proportion, say one half of the new shares. In this way the merchant bank makes sure the shares are placed with large investors before the actual date of issue comes round. Then, even if it is a bad day on the Stock Exchange when the shares are issued, the company's money is secure.

Another common method by which public companies raise share capital is by offering new shares for sale to the general public. The company's shares are advertised in leading newspapers and the public invited to apply.

The Official List and the Alternative Investment Market

Companies wishing to float on the London Stock Exchange have a choice of two markets, the Official List or the Alternative Investment Market (AIM).

Distinguish Between ...

The **Official List**, or main market is for established companies. There are now over 3,000 companies whose shares are traded on the Official List, and over 500 of these are non-UK based. Companies seeking to join the Official List must meet tough conditions to give investors confidence.

The **Alternative Investment Market** is a market for smaller companies that was established in 1995 to allow younger and growing businesses to raise capital to fund their growth. There are fewer rules for AIM but companies whose shares are quoted here are required to retain the assistance of a firm providing market expertise (known as the nominated adviser) at all times.

Companies can have their shares suspended from AIM if they fail to meet requirements. For example, in December 2001 the shares of Nottingham Forest Football Club were suspended because the club had failed to produce a set of accounts.

2.5 UNIT TRUSTS

Key Ideas 🔑

Spreading risks

Many individuals who invest on the Stock Exchange do not have enough money to buy a wide range of shares. They could lose money if the shares they hold drop in value. Unit trusts enable groups of investors to join together and pool their money to buy a wider range of shares, enabling the investors to receive a better rate of return on their investment.

- **Unit trusts** are managed by professional investors who buy a range of shares, thus spreading the risk.
- A **portfolio** is the list of shares held by the unit trust.
- **Trust funds** are legally owned by their managers but the benefit goes to the individual investors, who trust their managers to invest their money wisely.
- **Trust fund managers** control a number of trusts, each one of which has its own name; some trusts specialise in particular groups of shares, e.g. shares in British companies, shares in US companies, shares in particular sectors of the economy, shares in ethical businesses, etc.

Some unit trusts are designed to produce a regular income in the form of dividend yields, while others only produce money when they are sold, because their shares have risen in value considerably.

Some investors will therefore prefer a high yield while others prefer capital growth.

Growth is the increase in the value of the trust fund resulting from increases in share values.

Distinguish Between ...

Yield is the income which owners receive from their trust fund. Yield is expressed as the annual percentage return on each fund.

2.6 INVESTMENT TRUSTS

Key Ideas 🔑

Closed-ended funds

These are funds with a fixed number of issued shares.

Doctor Proctor outlines... THE NATURE OF INVESTMENT TRUSTS

Investment trusts are another form of organisation providing **long-term capital** for business. Without long-term funds it is impossible for companies to purchase expensive capital equipment, build new premises, expand into foreign markets, or acquire new businesses. An investment trust is a public limited company in its own right and is listed on the London Stock Exchange. As such it has an independent board that protects shareholders' interests and appoints the investment management company. Investors buy shares in the company. An investment trust is different from other companies like Cadbury-Schweppes or Tesco in that it does not make or sell physical goods. Instead, its sole purpose is to use shareholders' money to invest in the shares of other companies.

Investment trusts are **closed-ended funds**. This means that a fixed number of shares are issued at launch to raise the initial pool of investment capital. This initial pool of capital will increase or decrease according to how well it is invested. Typically, an investment trust will hold the shares of as many as 50 or 60 different companies at any one time and these will form part of its investment portfolio or assets. Investing in such a wide spread of different companies helps to minimise the risk to the investor.

Investor → Buys shares in → Investment trust → Buys shares in → 50 or 60 different companies

e.g. Foreign & Colonial Investment Trust

e.g. Virgin, BP, etc.

Investors gain from holding investment trusts in two ways:

1   They receive a **dividend**, which is their share of the profit earned by the investment trust in a given period, e.g. six months or a year.
2   The value of their investment grows, over time, particularly if their investment trust has invested for growth.

Shares in an investment trust are extremely affordable – investors can invest as little as a £250 lump sum or even invest monthly (some start at a mere £25 a month). Whilst in the short-term the Stock Market can be a volatile place, because investment trusts are concerned with the long-term they are well placed to ensure good rates of return over the longer period.

Many investors want to receive a high level of income from their money and have a lump sum to invest for this purpose. Some investment trusts are therefore organised so as to squeeze as much income out of their investment as possible. For example, High Income Investment Trusts invest the vast proportion of their assets in high yielding shares. Their priority is to generate a high and rising income stream.

Other investors are more concerned about the growth of their investment over time. If the companies that an investment trust invests in do well, the value of the investment portfolio will also grow and so should the value of the shares in the investment trust. There are at least 200 growth investment trusts to choose from.

2.7 TYPES OF SHARES

Key Ideas 🔑

Equity capital

There are two main types of share: ordinary and preference. Each offers different rights to dividends (returns) and capital repayment.

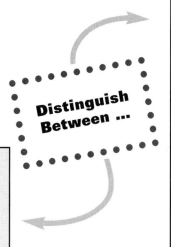

Distinguish Between ...

A **preference shareholder** is entitled to receive a dividend out of profits even when there may be insufficient profits to pay ordinary shareholders. However, they have few voting rights and hence less influence on company policy.

An **ordinary shareholder** shares in the profits of the business after all other investors have been paid their dues. The ordinary shareholder is able to vote at General Meetings of the company, including the appointment of the Board of Directors. The wealth of the company is owned by the ordinary shareholders and is referred to as **equity capital**.

Example

For example, JD Wetherspoon, which owns pubs throughout the UK, reported in its annual report and accounts for 2001 that its shareholdings were made up as follows:

Ordinary shareholdings at 29 July 2001

Shares of 2p each	Number of Shareholders	Shareholdings %	Number	Total shares held %
Up to 2,500	4,035	83.02	2,322,325	1.10
2,501 to 10,000	431	8.87	2,067,966	0.97
10,001 to 250,000	319	6.56	16,017,402	7.58
250,001 to 500,000	28	0.58	9,686,493	4.59
500,001 to 1,000,000	14	0.29	10,684,606	5.06
Over 1,000,000	33	0.68	170,432,351	80.70
	4,860	100	211,211,143	100

Note that the majority of shareholdings are small.

Note that the majority of shares are held by only 33 large shareholders.

An examination of information provided for shareholders in the annual report of J D Wetherspoon reveals that the largest shareholders are pension funds, investment trusts and insurance companies, the largest two of which each have about 10% of the shares.

Further examination of the Wetherspoon report for 2001 showed that the Board of Directors proposed (subject to the shareholders' consent) to pay a final dividend of 1.93p on 30 November 2001 to those shareholders on the share register at 28 September 2001, bringing the total dividend for the year to 2.93p.

2.7 TYPES OF SHARES

The return to preference shareholders is usually measured in percentage terms, e.g. eight per cent £1 preference shares would entitle the holder to 8p per year for each share held.

There are usually fewer preference shares than ordinary shares and some companies have none at all.

Typically the largest percentage of shares in public companies in this country is held by financial institutions although there are many small shareholders with a smaller number of shares.

The authorised capital of a company and the issued capital:

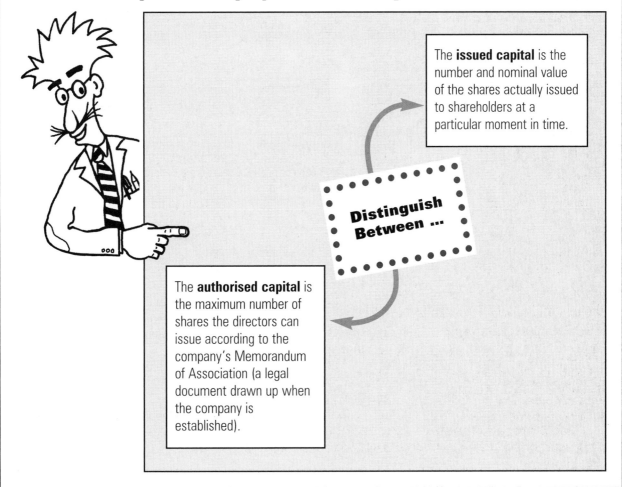

The **issued capital** is the number and nominal value of the shares actually issued to shareholders at a particular moment in time.

Distinguish Between ...

The **authorised capital** is the maximum number of shares the directors can issue according to the company's Memorandum of Association (a legal document drawn up when the company is established).

2.8 Sources of Third Party Finance

Key Ideas

Debentures

So far we have been examining the capital provided for companies by the shareholders. In addition, companies receive money from outside – i.e. third party finance.

Doctor Proctor outlines... Companies and Debentures

Large amounts of business finance are provided by investors who do not want to take the risk of becoming shareholders in a company. These third party investors include banks, insurance companies and pension funds who, for some of their investments at least, require stable income and greater security than they would receive from shareholdings.

The terms loan stock/debentures or company bonds are used to describe fixed interest third party loans to companies.

The basic principle of a debenture is that a loan is made to the company in accordance with terms set out in a certifying document. Typically, loan stock involves a fixed rate of interest and is repaid (redeemed) by the company on a predetermined date.

Sometimes loan stock is 'secured' on specified assets of the business in case the company runs into financial difficulties.

Example

An 8 per cent debenture of £100 dated 1 November 2010 requires the company to pay £8 a year to the debenture holder until 2010, when the capital sum of £100 must be repaid.

'Convertible' debentures are another attractive option for investors as they can be converted into shares at some future date and at a predetermined price. Debenture holders therefore have fixed income in the short term with the possibility of capital gains at low risk in the long term.

There is a range of other forms of third party finance to companies including:

- bank loans
- overdrafts
- mortgages
- hire purchase
- trade credit, etc.

Section 2.1: What is a Company?

Explain the difference between the following:

- A public company and a private company.
- Ltd and plc.
- A sole trader and a partnership.
- Limited and unlimited liability.

Section 2.2: Controlling the Activities of Companies

State whether the following information would appear in the Articles or the Memorandum of Association:

- Details of how long directors are allowed to retain their directorship.
- The voting rights of shareholders.
- A statement of company objectives.
- Amounts of different types of shares invested in the company.
- An outline of how the chairperson of the company will be appointed.
- Details of the Annual General Meeting of the company.
- The registered office of the company.

Section 2.3: The Role of Directors

State which of the following are true and which are false:

1 The chair of a company is the same person as the managing director.
2 Only executive directors are responsible for the stewardship of the company.
3 Non-executive directors can play a role in removing the managing director.
4 Shareholders' vote on the re-appointment of the Board.
5 Shareholders voting rights are often proportionate to the number of shares they hold.
6 Corporate governance is the system by which companies are directed and controlled.

Section 2.4: The Role of the Stock Exchange

1 What is the name of the body responsible for overseeing the work of the Stock Exchange?

2 Where are the informational requirements about seeking a listing on the Stock Exchange set out?
3 What organisations will help to arrange for the shares of a company to 'go public'?
4 How does 'placing' shares reduce the risk involved with introducing them to the Stock Exchange?
5 What is the difference between the Official List and the Alternative Investment Market?

Section 2.5: Unit Trusts

How does the purchase of units in a unit trust enable an investor to spread their risk? What is the difference between yield and growth in the context of a unit trust?

Section 2.6: Investment Trusts

How might an individual purchase shares in an investment trust? What would be the advantages of investing in this way?

Section 2.7: Types of Shares

Which of the following statements are true and which are false?

1 A company quoted on the Stock Exchange benefits because it becomes easier to raise more funds as a market already exists for the company's shares.
2 An ordinary shareholder shares in the profits of the business before other investors are paid their dues.
3 The capital provided by preference shareholders is called equity.
4 The issued share capital of a company is the maximum amount that the company is allowed to raise.
5 The directors of a company are responsible to the shareholders for the performance of the company.

Section 2.8: Sources of Third Party Finance

Describe the following:

1 Debentures
2 Convertible loan stock

This unit identifies the principal ingredients of company reports while alerting the reader to be aware that different companies will present reports and financial information in different ways. This depends on the type of business they are involved in and the extent to which they are prepared to divulge information.

Topics covered in this unit

3.1 The Main Components of Company Reports

Outlines the nature and importance of company reports, setting out the key bodies that govern the pattern of company reports. In addition there is a list of the key components of a company report.

3.2 Financial Highlights

Company reports typically start out with a number of financial highlights designed to attract the interest and commitment of investors.

3.3 The Chairperson and Chief Executive's Report

The chair and chief executive have a key role in communicating with shareholders and wider stakeholder groupings. This section of the report discusses the company or group's general performance and comments on events during the trading year. Future prospects are also discussed.

3.4 Directors' Report and Corporate Governance Report

Directors are legally bound by the Companies Act to report to shareholders and have a responsibility to do so in order to retain a Stock Exchange Listing. The directors are required to produce financial statements and a review of operations. As a result of the Cadbury Committee on Corporate Governance, companies are also required to set out the internal controls, directors' responsibilities, and other aspects of the internal organisation of the company.

3.5 Auditing Company Reports

Sets out the role of auditors in checking on the authenticity of company reports.

3.6 The Main Types of Financial Statements

Lists the main types of financial statements that are required in a company report and which are covered in greater detail in Unit 4 of the book.

Questions

3.1 THE MAIN COMPONENTS OF COMPANY REPORTS

Key Ideas

Accountability

Being **accountable** means being responsible for actions and conduct. Over the years there has been increasing pressure on organisations to be accountable to their stakeholders. Being accountable involves setting out in a clear and fair way exactly what the company does and how it is performing. In many companies, in the twenty-first century this goes well beyond providing financial information to include the provision of environmental audits, details of trading policies, relationships with employees and many other areas.

The main way in which companies communicate with their stakeholders today is through the publication of an annual report and accounts (the **financial statements**).

Legal requirements

Legal requirements are set out by various **Companies Acts.** Every company must present an annual report to shareholders and submit a copy to Companies House. This must be done within ten months of the year-end for a private limited company, and within seven months of the year-end in the case of a plc.

Content of company reports

The annual report must include:

- a directors' report
- an auditor's report
- a profit and loss account
- a balance sheet
- a cash flow statement
- a statement of total gains and losses
- notes to provide further information about the accounts.

The directors are responsible for the preparation of the accounts which must give a **true and fair view**.

What information must be produced in an annual report?

The requirements of what should be included in company reports are set out by four main sources:

- **1.** Legal requirements
- **2.** Accounting standards

Requirements governing content and layout of company reports

- **3.** Stock Exchange rules
- **4.** Codes of best practice for corporate governance

Dr Proctor says:

'You Must Know This!'

A true and fair view is one where the accounts reflect what has actually happened and do not mislead the reader. They must meet a number of important **accounting standards.**

Directors must prepare accounts for every UK company. In addition, if a company is a **parent company** then it must produce group accounts providing consolidated balance sheets and profit and loss accounts.

3.1 THE MAIN COMPONENTS OF COMPANY REPORTS

Format of company reports

The formats in which financial reports must be presented are prescribed. Some minor variations are allowed if the 'users' understanding is improved as a result'. There are a small number of alternative formats that can be chosen.

Accounting standards

Financial reports contained in the annual report are subject to **Financial Reporting Standards (FRSs)** and the older **Statements of Standard Accounting Practice (SSAPs)** which are now gradually being replaced.

FRSs are issued by the **Accounting Standards Board**, which reports to the independent **Financial Reporting Council**, the body which represents accountants and users of accounts.

Stock Exchange Rules

Companies listed on the London Stock Exchange must also comply with the requirements on reporting laid down in The Listing Rules (set out in the Yellow Book). These require companies to produce interim reports (i.e. at six month intervals). The informational requirements of the Stock Exchange are broadly similar to those set out by the Companies Act and accounting standards. All listed companies must state in their annual report that they are complying with the code of practice on corporate governance established as a result of the Cadbury Report.

Corporate Governance: Codes of Best Practice

The **Cadbury Committee** report published in December 1992 set out a code of best practice designed 'to achieve the necessary high standards of corporate behaviour'.

The Code requires Boards to report on the responsibilities of directors in relation to the preparation of accounts and the effectiveness of the company's internal control procedures and to present a balanced and understandable assessment of the company's position.

In 1995 the **Greenbury Committee** drew up a further code of best practice setting out guidelines for determining and reporting on directors' pay.

More on accounting standards

Dr Proctor says:
'You Must Know This!'

Accounting standards are rules and regulations governing the measurement and/or disclosure of particular types of transactions – for example, creating a standard for accounting for the depreciation of machinery and other assets.

The purpose of accounting standards is to create common ways of reporting which meet internationally acceptable standards. The aim is to try and make sure that there are consistent ways of reporting company performance so that accurate comparisons can be made between the performance of one company and another, as well as comparisons of the same company's performance over time.

3.1 THE MAIN COMPONENTS OF COMPANY REPORTS

Doctor Proctor outlines... AUDITORS AND THE REGULATORY FRAMEWORK

The role of auditors

Shareholders appoint **auditors** to assess whether the accounts give a 'true and fair' view of the company's position. Auditors are required to review the business's accounting records, current operations and future prospects. In addition, the **Financial Reporting Review Panel** checks annual reports for compliance with legislation and FRSs.

Financial Reporting: the Regulatory Framework

Who makes the rules

- Government
- Accountancy profession
- Financial community
- Stock Exchange

→ Financial Reporting Council

→ Accounting Standards Board

Regulations

- Companies Acts
- Accounting Standards – FRSS, SSAPs
- Stock Exchange Listing Rules

→ Annual Report

Compliance (how the rules are enforced)

- Auditors
- Financial Reporting Review Panel
- Shareholders

3.2 FINANCIAL HIGHLIGHTS

Key Ideas 🔑

Financial highlights

The financial highlights of a company typically show those financial indicators that have been particularly good in the previous year.

Doctor Proctor outlines... THE SIGNIFICANCE OF THE FINANCIAL HIGHLIGHTS PAGE

Typically, the opening page of a company report will set out the financial highlights of the previous year. The purpose of this section is to highlight to the investor those financial and other indicators that have been particularly pleasing.

Many company reports also set out a five year summary in their financial highlights section showing changes in turnover, profits, dividends, etc. over a five year period.

Example

Holmes Place plc, a major upmarket European Health and Leisure Club operator, included in its financial highlights for 2000:

- Turnover up 43% to £87.7 million (£61.4 million in 1999)
- Operating profit up 49% to £15.9 million (£10.6 million in 1999)
- Earnings per share increased by 39% to 14.6 pence (10.5 pence in 1999)
- Total membership of 191,316 (130,109 in 1999) an increase of 47%.

These figures show an increase in:

- the value of sales (turnover)
- profit (operating profit)
- profit relative to the value of shares (earnings per share)
- the number of Holmes Place members.

3.3 THE CHAIRPERSON AND CHIEF EXECUTIVE'S REPORT

Where the chair and the chief executive of a company are separated, as recommended by the Cadbury Report, the annual report may include both a Chairperson's Statement and a Chief Executive's Review.

The **Chairperson's Statement** is not a legal requirement but it provides a good opportunity for the chair of a company to present the company in a positive light to investors and to a wider financial audience, including the financial press and other media. The Chair's Statement needs to be cautiously optimistic – it needs to present the company in a positive light but not push expectations of the company's performance above a sustainable level.

The Chairperson's Statement sets out a summary of key successes for the previous year and outlines the payment of the dividend that the Board is proposing to pay to shareholders.

Example

The Chairperson's Statement for Holmes Place in 1990 set out that:

'During the year, we opened eight clubs in the UK and five in continental Europe, including the acquisition of Alma Sports Club in Dusseldorf, and by the end of 2000 operated from 52 clubs; 39 in the UK and 13 in continental Europe.'

The report went on to state:

'The Board recommends a final dividend of 3.0 pence per share. Together with the interim dividend (half year) of 1.65 pence paid in November, this makes a total dividend for the year of 4.65 pence.'

The **Chief Executive's Review** is not a legal requirement. As would be expected, this review gives a more detailed outline of the strategy and running of the company so that shareholders can get a better picture of a company's ongoing direction. The **strategy** is the long-term planning of the company, involving substantial resources.

The Chief Executive's Review will outline the key parts of the organisation and its successes and weak areas, including outlining acquisitions by the company and parts that have been sold off. Reading this review will give readers a better understanding of the scope of activities involved and will indicate what to look out for in terms of future prospects.

Example

The Chief Executive's Review for Holmes Place set out that:

'Our strategy is to create shareholder value by being the leading European premium health and fitness club operator. To achieve this, we are pursuing a strategy of concentrating our expansion in carefully targeted cities in the UK and our chosen regions in Central Europe and the Iberian Peninsula.'

The review went on to outline the strength of operations in London and the South-East, the opening of new clubs including those in Milton Keynes, Kensington and Nottingham. It showed that existing clubs in Continental Europe, such as those in Switzerland, were successful and that new clubs were opening up in locations such as in Lisbon and Porto. The review also highlighted the success of leisure management operations in running and opening up new hotels.

Finally, the review painted a picture of a healthy future with ongoing increases in membership.

3.4 DIRECTORS' REPORT AND CORPORATE GOVERNANCE REPORT

Doctor Proctor outlines... THE IMPORTANCE OF THE DIRECTORS' REPORT

The **Directors' Report** is a legal obligation required by the Companies Act. In addition, the Stock Exchange Listing also requires directors to provide information to keep shareholders up to date with current developments. The Directors' Report traditionally included details about corporate governance – but following the Cadbury Commission a substantial amount of this information has been transferred to a separate section in the report on corporate governance.

This list in the Directors' Report for Holmes Place is representative of the types of information that you will find in the Directors' Report of any public company.

Example

The Directors' Report for Holmes Place 2000 is typical of many Directors' Reports, providing information on the following:

- A statement of the principal activity of the Group – i.e. the operation of health and fitness clubs.
- A statement of key results – i.e. profits (and where the profit and loss account can be found in the report).
- A statement of proposed dividends to be paid to shareholders.
- A review of the business and future developments (set out in the Chairman's and Chief Executive's Statements).
- A list of executive and non-executive directors.
- A list of substantial shareholdings in the company (groups and individuals with 3 per cent or more of the shares).
- A statement about the importance of employees in the organisation.
- A statement about the importance of the company's environmental policy.
- A statement about the importance of the creditor payment policy (paying creditors within an agreed time).
- A statement giving a breakdown of the share capital of the company.
- A statement setting out the name of the auditors of the company.

3.4 DIRECTORS' REPORT AND CORPORATE GOVERNANCE REPORT

Doctor Proctor outlines... THE IMPORTANCE OF THE CORPORATE GOVERNANCE REPORT

We have already seen that in this country there has been an increasing emphasis on demonstrating transparently the ways in which companies are organised and managed. Investors and other stakeholders have a right to know about the working and practices of companies. In addition, the financial affairs of a company need to be open to scrutiny.

The Cadbury Committee set out a **Code of Practice on Corporate Governance** and all listed companies are expected to make a statement in their report and accounts about their compliance with the Code (and identify any areas of non-compliance). This Code has been consolidated by the more recent Greenbury and Hampel Committees.

Reports on corporate governance therefore must comply with the Combined Code on Corporate Governance referred to as 'the Code'.

Therefore a report will typically include the following sections:

1 A statement that 'the Code' is being applied.

2 A section setting out **internal controls** within a group/company. This section outlines who will be responsible for risk management within the company, and how risks will be minimised, including a statement of how executive directors and managers will control the key functions of the business. It also specifies the way in which budgeting will be monitored and controlled and other relevant aspects of internal control to minimise risk.

3 A section setting out the **purpose and structure of the Board of Directors** and its role in controlling the company. This will include an outline of the main committees set out by the Board, including the Audit Committee, the Remuneration Committee, and

the Nomination Committee (for nominating new directors). The Cadbury Committee set out that the Board of Directors 'must meet regularly, retain full and effective control over the company and monitor the executive management'. Non-executive directors are expected to bring to a company the quality of independent judgement. The service contracts of executive directors should not normally exceed three years.

4 A section setting out the **remuneration** of directors and the group or company's policy on directors' remuneration.

5 A section setting out **relationships with shareholders**, i.e. the nature of and times of meetings and communications with shareholders.

6 A section setting out the **auditing arrangements** for the company, including the make-up of the Audit Committee, as well as the directors' responsibilities for financial statements. The Audit Committee should consist of at least three non-executive directors.

7 A section setting out the composition of the **nomination committee** for new directors.

8 A statement that after careful consideration the directors are happy that the group or company is a **going concern**, i.e. that it has adequate resources to continue to operate into the foreseeable future.

9 **A statement of compliance** setting out that the company is in full compliance with 'the Code', as set out by the Financial Services Authority.

3.5 AUDITING COMPANY REPORTS

Dr Proctor says:
'You Must Know This!'

An auditor is an independent accountant who scrutinises the financial statements of a company to check and hopefully to verify that the financial statements and accounts provide a true and fair record.

The key elements of an auditor's report on financial statements are:

1 A title identifying the persons to whom the report is addressed, namely the shareholders.

2 An introductory paragraph setting out the financial statements that have been audited.

4 Auditor's signature and date.

3 Sections setting out:

(i) the responsibilities of directors and auditors

(ii) the basis of the auditor's opinion

(iii) the auditor's opinion.

Example

For example, the Auditor's Report for Holmes Place in 2000:

1 was addressed to the members of Holmes Place plc

2 identified the accounting statements that had been audited, including the balance sheet and the profit and loss account

3 (i) set out that directors were responsible for preparing the annual report, including financial statements with regard to UK law and financial standards. It stated that the auditors were responsible for checking that financial statements provide an accurate and fair picture and whether appropriate information had been provided to the auditors by the company. It also set out that the auditors are responsible for checking that the company had provided appropriate information about corporate governance, directors' remuneration, etc.

(ii) set out that the auditor's opinion is based on auditing standards issued by the Auditing Standards Board

(iii) Stated that 'in our opinion the financial statements give a true and fair view of the state of affairs of the Company and the Group as at 31 December 2000'

4 was signed by Deloitte & Touche, Chartered Accountants and Registered Auditors.

3.6 THE MAIN TYPES OF FINANCIAL STATEMENTS

Key Ideas 🔑

Financial statements in company reports

Financial statements provide a financial record of performance and must appear in company reports.

Doctor Proctor outlines... FINANCIAL STATEMENTS

1 The profit and loss account

2 The balance sheet

The key financial statements which are included in a company report are:

3 The cash flow statement

4 Other primary statements.

There will then follow an outline of the accounting policies that have been used.

Finally, there is a set of notes to the financial statements providing further detail to the reader.

Section 3.1: The Main Components of Company Reports

1 What are the four main sources of requirements governing the content and layout of company reports?
2 List five major items which must appear in a company report.

Section 3.2: Financial Highlights

The following table shows a five-year summary of some key financial indicators for Pizza Express plc up to 2001.

	2001	2000	1999	1998	1997
Group turnover (£m)	185.6	150.1	126.6	99.6	71.1
Profit before tax (£m)	40.0	32.2	28.7	22.5	15.6
Dividends (pence)	8.4	6.7	5.4	4.25	3.35

Why might shareholders be pleased with the information shown above?

Section 3.3: The Chairperson and Chief Executive's Report

1 Is the Chairperson's Statement a legal requirement? Is the Chief Executive's Report a legal requirement?
2 Why should these statements be neither pessimistic nor too optimistic?
3 Who else is likely to read these statements and reports in addition to investors?

Section 3.4: Directors' Report and Corporate Governance Report

The following statement is taken from the report of a well known company:

> The Board currently comprises four executive and three independent non-executive Directors. Each Director submits for re-election at least every three years. Directors who are appointed during the year are subject to re-appointment by the Shareholders at the next Annual General Meeting. There is a clear delineation of responsibility between the Chairperson and the Chief Executive and other executive Directors. There are ten regular Board meetings each year and other ad hoc meetings are held as required to direct overall Group strategy and operations.

1 In which section of the company report would you expect to find the above statement?
2 Is it a legal requirement for companies to produce a directors' report?
3 What is meant by accountability? How does a statement on corporate governance help to improve accountability?

Section 3.5: Auditing Company Reports

What are the four key elements of an Auditor's Report?

Section 3.6: The Main Types of Financial Statements

List three major types of financial statements which must be produced by companies in their reports.

UNIT 4

FINANCIAL STATEMENTS AND ACCOUNTS

Topics covered in this unit

This section examines each of the key financial statements which companies need to produce in their reports to shareholders.

4.1 The Profit and Loss Account

The profit and loss account gives a breakdown of the profit or loss made by a company in a given trading period, e.g. six months or one year. It shows the value of the sales made by the organisation, and the cost of making these sales, and then identifies what happens to the profit or loss made in that trading period.

4.2 The Balance Sheet

The balance sheet is like a photograph of a company's financial position at a particular instant in time. The balance sheet contains two sections – a list of the company's assets and a summary of its liabilities and capital.

4.3 The Cash Flow Statement

The cash flow statement sets out actual cash receipts and payments during a particular period of time, e.g. one year. It shows how the main categories of cash flow have changed the cash balance in particular periods.

4.4 Notes to the Accounts

Notes to the accounts provide more detail of the various items which have appeared in the profit and loss account, balance sheet, and cash flow statement. They also set out the accounting policies adopted by the company.

4.5 Reporting Business Changes

If the company has acquired or terminated business activities, or has experienced some other unusual circumstance, this will need to be clearly highlighted.

4.6 The Auditor's Opinion

The auditor must set out in the company report their opinion on whether the accounts represent a true and fair view of the state of affairs of the company.

4.7 Financial Statements Summary

Questions

4.1 THE PROFIT AND LOSS ACCOUNT

Key Ideas

Components of a profit and loss account

The profit and loss account gives a breakdown of how the profit or loss made by a company is arrived at.

Doctor Proctor outlines...

Profit and loss accounts are allowed to be presented in one of four different formats – in this book we concentrate on the most typical format.

The profit or loss of the company is made as a result of the company making items which it sells,

producing a service, or from trading, i.e. buying in items and then selling them at a higher price. In order to work out profit we need to take away from the value of the sales the cost of making those sales and the expenses of running the business.

The following table shows the Group Profit and Loss Account for Thistle Hotels plc for the financial year ended 31 December 2000. (Note that negative figures appear in brackets.)

	Notes	£m	
Turnover	1	324.6	
Cost of sales		(196.8)	
Gross profit	1	127.8	How profit was generated, i.e. revenue – cost of sales and expenses
Administrative expenses		22.4	
Operating profit	2	105.4	
Profit on sale of tangible fixed assets		1.2	
Interest payable and similar charges		(38.4)	
Profit before taxation		68.2	
Taxation		(13.4)	
Profit for the financial year (after tax)		54.8	Appropriation of profits
Dividends		(24.6)	
Profit retained		30.2	

The **upper section** of the profit and loss account shows how profit was generated:

- **Turnover** refers to the value of the sales or revenue made by Thistle Hotels during the course of the year: for example, receipts from guests staying in the hotels, dinners and other functions paid for by customers, etc.

- **Cost of sales** refers to the costs incurred **directly** in creating the turnover. For example, it will include the cost of the ingredients that go into providing meals in the hotel, the wages directly paid to staff for cleaning the rooms, waiting on tables, etc.

4.1 THE PROFIT AND LOSS ACCOUNT

- **Gross profit** is calculated by deducting the value of the cost of sales from the value of the turnover (£m): (324.6-196.8 = 127.8).

- **Expenses** need to be deducted from gross profit to arrive at a figure for **operating profit**. In the example of Thistle Hotels, expenses are the administrative costs of running the hotel business. These overhead costs cannot be directly related to the turnover of the business: for example, senior managers' wages need to be paid irrespective of the level of occupancy of the hotels.

The **lower section** shows how profit has been appropriated between corporation tax paid to the Inland Revenue, dividends paid to shareholders and the retention of profits in the business. Profits retained in the business add to the wealth of the business and can be used to grow the business, e.g. for investing in or purchasing other businesses, buying new plants and equipment, etc.

Notes to the accounts: this column identifies a series of notes which give more details and which can be found in a separate section of the company report.

Some businesses do not make a profit each year and this is represented as a loss in the profit and loss account. For example, a number of well known football clubs sometimes show a loss.

Key Ideas

Loss

For example, an extract from the Profit and Loss Account for Leicester City Football Club for the year ended 31 July 2000 showed (in £000):

Turnover	26,038
Cost of sales	(30,019)
Gross loss	(3,981)
Administrative expenses	(3,313)
Operating loss	(7,294)

Leading football clubs find it difficult to make regular profits because the cost of players wages (a key element of the cost of sales) is so high.

The turnover of a Premier League football club typically comes from sales of season and other tickets, television rights, sponsorship deals and sales of merchandise. Clubs who manage to retain a position in the Premier League benefit enormously from television rights. However, when a club is relegated this source of income is massively reduced. As a result, clubs relegated from the Premier to the First Division see their turnover drastically reduced while their cost of sales (largely consisting of players' wages) remains high, creating a very high loss for the club.

This is well illustrated by the plight of Nottingham Forest Football Club which was relegated from the Premier Division at the end of the 1999 season.

Extract from Consolidated Profit and Loss Account for Nottingham Forest Football Club

	2000 £000	1999 £000
Turnover	9,484	17,033
External charges	(3,344)	(3,928)
Staff costs including signing-on fees	(10,928)	(11,806)
Gross profit/loss	(4,778)	1,269
Depreciation and amortisation of players' registrations	(5,352)	(5,352)
Operating loss	(10,130)	(2,783)

The account shows that in 2000 the club made a much bigger operating loss than in 1999. In 1999 it was also able to receive substantial sums of money from the sale of players (not shown in the extract), enabling the company to make an overall profit of nearly £8 million, compared with 1999 when it made a loss of nearly £12 million.

4.2 THE BALANCE SHEET

Key Ideas 🔑

Assets and liabilities

If you were asked 'What is the value of your personal wealth at this moment in time?' a good reply would be 'the value of those things that I own and the money that is owed to me minus what I owe to other people'. The same is true of a company.

To understand the financial position of the business, it is necessary to 'freeze' the values of financial components at a certain point in time. These values, or **balances**, are used to construct a balance sheet.

A balance sheet shows the relationship between the **assets** of the business (what the business owns or is owed), and the **liabilities** of the business (what the business owes).

When we take away the liabilities from the assets this gives a figure for **net assets**, which shows how much the business is worth at a moment in time.

The value for net assets will be the same value as that of the **shareholders' capital** because shareholders own the business. If you asked shareholders 'how much is your company worth at this moment in time?' they would reply 'the value of the net assets!'

Doctor Proctor outlines... WHY BALANCE SHEETS BALANCE

A balance sheet simply shows that:

Capital of the business = Assets – Liabilities

Because this is an equation it can also be arranged as:

Assets = Capital + Liabilities

The structure of a balance sheet
The example on the right shows the basic structure of a balance sheet.

The category headings are often made up of several individual balances, for example, creditors due within one year may include figures for trade credit, bank overdrafts and other creditors such as tax owed to government agencies. In published accounts, the balance sheet will include comparative figures for the previous year and 'notes to the accounts' to explain the composition of individual balances.

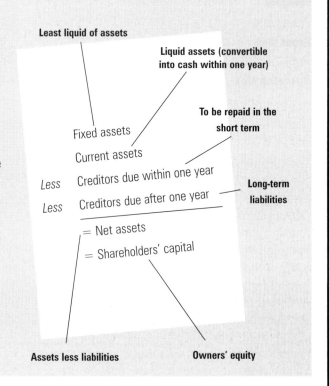

4.2 THE BALANCE SHEET

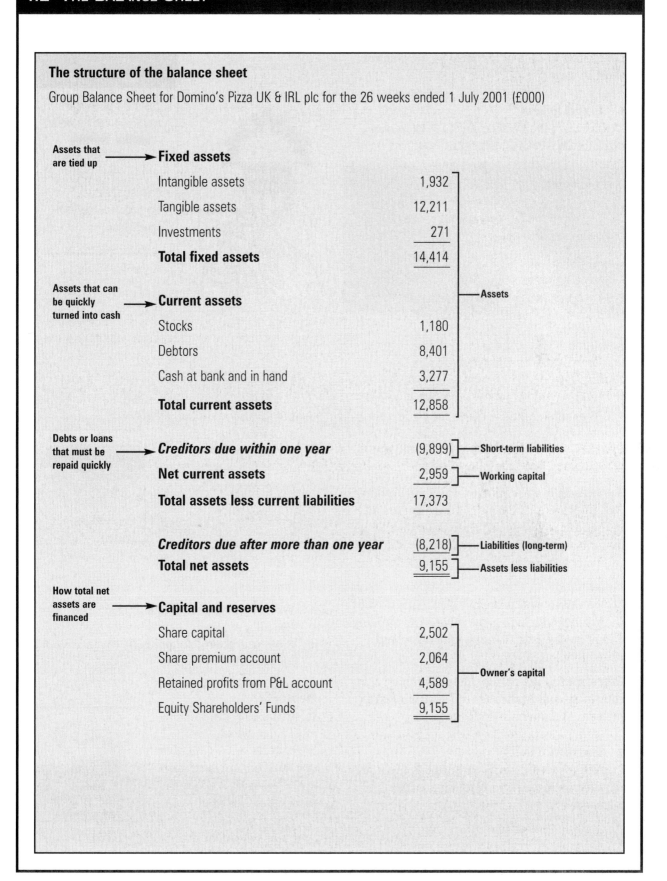

The structure of the balance sheet

Group Balance Sheet for Domino's Pizza UK & IRL plc for the 26 weeks ended 1 July 2001 (£000)

Fixed assets _(Assets that are tied up)_	
Intangible assets	1,932
Tangible assets	12,211
Investments	271
Total fixed assets	14,414
Current assets _(Assets that can be quickly turned into cash)_	
Stocks	1,180
Debtors	8,401
Cash at bank and in hand	3,277
Total current assets	12,858
Creditors due within one year _(Debts or loans that must be repaid quickly)_ — Short-term liabilities	(9,899)
Net current assets — Working capital	2,959
Total assets less current liabilities	17,373
Creditors due after more than one year — Liabilities (long-term)	(8,218)
Total net assets — Assets less liabilities	9,155
Capital and reserves _(How total net assets are financed)_	
Share capital	2,502
Share premium account	2,064
Retained profits from P&L account	4,589
Equity Shareholders' Funds	9,155

Assets · _Owner's capital_

4.2 THE BALANCE SHEET

Let us look at each of the parts of the balance sheet in turn:

1 Fixed assets

Extract from the balance sheet for Domino's Pizza for 26 weeks ended 1 July 2001

Fixed assets	
Intangible assets	1,932
Tangible assets	12,211
Investments	271
Total fixed assets	14,414

Dr Proctor says:
'You Must Know This!'

There are three main types of current assets – **stocks**, **debtors** and **cash**. They appear in that order in the balance sheet – starting with the least liquid stock.

Domino's Pizza plc is the market leader in the fast-growing pizza delivery market in this country. It prides itself on a system consisting of the three elements: product, service and image.

Fixed assets are the 'tools of the trade' that enable a business to generate wealth, and to function on a day-to-day basis. They are not purchased for resale to the customer.

The **intangible assets** are non-physical things which enhance the wealth of the business and in the case of Domino's Pizza would include its brand name and the positive image of the company – these are real assets that help it to generate ongoing wealth.

The **tangible assets** are physical items used by the business, including the value of its buildings and premises, pizza making machinery and equipment, etc.

Investments are shareholdings in other companies and in the case of Domino's Pizza include investment in joint ventures.

2 Current assets

Current assets are assets that arise from, or are required for, the everyday trading of the business.

In practice, any asset that is not a fixed asset is a current asset.

- **Liquidity** is the ease with which an asset can be turned into cash. Cash is obviously the most liquid of all assets.

- **Stocks** consist of costs involved in providing goods or services to customers. There are three categories of stocks for manufactured goods:

Stocks

i. **Raw materials** are goods in their original state purchased from outside suppliers – e.g. coal, iron ore, etc.
ii. **Work-in-progress** refers to goods that are not fully made.
iii. **Finished goods** are products that are ready for sale.

Debtors

In commercial transactions most sales are on credit – typically 30 or 60 days after sale. Debtors are customers at the business who have taken goods on credit.

Debtors
(= IOUs for goods sold on credit)

4.2 THE BALANCE SHEET

Cash

Cash is a current asset because it is a resource that helps the business to meet its obligations to suppliers and employees in the short term.

Cash

Doctor Proctor Calculates

You can calculate the total value of current assets by adding together the various items shown here.

Illustration of a 'current assets' section of company accounts for Domino's Pizza for 26 weeks ended 1 July 2001:

	£000
Current assets	
Stocks	1,180
Debtors	8,401
Cash	3,277
Total current assets	12,858

3 Current liabilities

An **asset** is an amount OWED TO the business.

Distinguish Between ...

A **liability** is an amount OWED BY the business.

Businesses owe money because they have built up liabilities in the past.

Dr Proctor says:
'You Must Know This!'

Financial reports distinguish between liabilities that fall due in less than one year, and those that fall due in more than one year. Liabilities which fall due in less than one year are called **current liabilities**.

On 1 July 2001 Domino's Pizza had current liabilities of £9,899,000. This figure appeared in the balance sheet in brackets to show that it was a liability, i.e. a negative figure.

Current liabilities consist of liabilities for bank overdrafts, unpaid corporation tax, goods and supplies received on credit, a proposed dividend to shareholders that has not yet been paid, etc.

In Domino's balance sheet this appeared as:

Creditors:	£000
Amounts falling due within one year	(9,899)

4.2 THE BALANCE SHEET

4 Net current assets

The figure for net current assets which appears in a balance sheet is a very important one because it shows how solvent the company is.

Solvency is the ability of a company to pay its short-term debts and running costs such as its wage bill and the ability to buy in raw materials.

Sometimes the term **working capital** is used rather than net current assets. This is a useful descriptive term because it describes the capital that the company has to work with at a particular moment in time.

Doctor Proctor Calculates

Working capital (net current assets) is simply calculated by taking away current liabilities from current assets. You can see how this works in the case of Domino's Pizza for the 26 weeks ended 1 July 2001:

Current assets	£000
Stocks	1,180
Debtors	8,401
Cash	3,277
Total current assets	12,858
Creditors	
Amounts falling due within one year	(9,899)
Net current assets	2,959

Long-term liabilities would include items such as bank loans and hire purchase and lease arrangements.

5 Total assets less current liabilities

The next figure that appears in the balance sheet is a calculation of the total assets minus just the current liabilities.

Continuing the case of Domino's Pizza we can summarise this information from the balance sheet in the following way:

	£000
Total fixed assets	14,414
Total current assets	12,858
Current liabilities	(9,899)
Total assets less current liabilities	17,373

6 Net assets of the business

The net assets of a business shows the assets of the business minus all forms of liability at a particular moment in time. It is a good indicator of how much the business is worth, based on the notion that an organisation is worth its assets minus its liabilities.

To find out the net assets from a balance sheet we simply take away long-term liabilities from the figure for **total assets less current liabilities**.

In the case of Domino's Pizza for the 26 weeks ended 1 July 2001 this was:

	£000
Total assets less current liabilities	17,373
Creditors	
Amounts falling due after more than one year	(8,218)
Net assets	9,155

4.2 THE BALANCE SHEET

7   Capital and reserves

The final section of the balance sheet shows the shareholders' funds because it is the shareholders of a company that are the owners of the net assets of the business.

For example, if at the 1 July 2001 the net assets of Domino's Pizza are worth more than they were a year earlier then shareholders' capital will have risen by the same amount.

Dr Proctor says:
'You Must Know This!'

Equity shareholders' funds (owners' capital) must always be equal in value to the net assets of the business.

We can illustrate the balance between net assets and equity shareholders' funds by taking the example of Domino's Pizza at 1 July 2001:

	£000
Net assets	9,155
Capital and reserves	
Called up share capital	2,502
Share premium account	2,064
Profit and loss account	4,589
Equity shareholders' funds	9,155

Shareholders' funds are represented in the balance sheet in different ways, depending on how they have occurred.

Amounts in respect of issued share capital are broken up into two parts – the nominal value and the share premium.

The share premium is the difference between the amount raised and the nominal value when new shares are raised.

In the case of Domino's Pizza this appears as:

	£000
Called up share capital	2,502
Share premium account	2,064

In addition, realised profits and losses, net of dividend payments, are accumulated in the profit and loss account. The figure that appears in the balance sheet under the heading Profit and Loss Account is the accumulated balance of profits (or losses). It is made up of the accumulated balance brought forward from the previous year, to which is added the current year's balance.

The business can use these retained profits to fund further growth without having to raise new finance from external sources.

In the case of Domino's Pizza at 1 July 2001, it had accumulated £4,589,000 in the profit and loss account – funds which are available to finance growth.

A business like Domino's Pizza has capital which has been contributed by its owners. It can also add to its capital internally by using profits in order to finance growth.

4.3 THE CASH FLOW STATEMENT

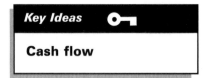

Key Ideas

Cash flow

Dr Proctor says:

'You Must Know This!'

Don't bother too much with the details of the cash flow statement – you simply need to have an understanding of its main purpose, and the main categories of cash flow.

The cash flow statement simply sets out the inflows and outflows of cash into a business in a particular period of time e.g. a year, half-year, etc. It shows how the main categories of cash flow have changed the cash balance in particular periods.

The following cash flow statement shows cash flow for the Bass Group for the year ended 30 September 2000. The Bass Group is made up of a range of hotels, clubs, pubs and other leisure interests.

Studying the cash flow statement shows that typical outflows of cash include payments for taxation, dividend payments, payments for the purchase of fixed assets such as new hotels, etc. Cash inflows include cash received from operating activities, payment for the disposal of fixed assets, etc.

The main categories of cash flow are:

1 **Net cash flow from operating activities.** This consists of the receipts and payments arising from the company's business activities. Note that the cash flow from operating activities for the Bass Group had risen from £986m in 1999 to £1,103m in 2000, showing a higher level of trading activity.

2 **Return on investment and servicing of finance.** This is calculated as interest received minus interest paid. It shows to what extent debt finance is a burden on the business. Note that in 1999 and 2000 the Bass Group had to pay out more under this heading than it received (minus £142m in 2000 and minus £135m in 1999).

3 **Taxation.** This represents payments of corporation tax made during the accounting period.

4 **Capital expenditure and financial investment** – i.e. the sum spent on fixed assets. Comparing this figure with the depreciation charge in the profit and loss account will give important pointers to future investment.

If the depreciation charge equates with the replacements spend required to maintain the average age and serviceability of fixed assets, then a higher spend would benefit the business and increase its capacity to generate profits.

A lower spend will have the opposite effect.

5 **Acquisitions.** This is the amount paid to acquire non-cash assets when buying other businesses. The figures show a higher emphasis on acquisitions in 2000 than in 1999.

6 **Equity dividends.** Payments to shareholders, e.g. £285m in 2000.

7 **Net cash flow.** This shows the difference between cash coming into the company mainly from operating activities and cash outflows from paying interest, dividends, tax, etc. The figure for Bass is £1,732m.

8 **Financing.** Amounts raised from, or repaid to investors in the company. For example, repaying bank loans or raising fresh finance through an issue of shares.

4.3 THE CASH FLOW STATEMENT

Bass Group cash flow statement

	2000 £m	2000 £m	1999 £m	1999 £m
Operating activities		1,103		986
Dividends received from associates		11		10
Interest paid	(191)		(174)	
Dividends paid to minority shareholders	(4)		(4)	
Dividends paid to non-equity shareholders	(1)		(1)	
Interest received	54		44	
Return on investments and servicing of finance		(142)		(135)
UK corporation tax paid	(101)		(138)	
Overseas corporate tax paid	(57)		(36)	
Taxation		(158)		(174)
Paid: Tangible fixed assets	(686)	(656)		
Trade loans	(39)	(60)		
Other fixed asset investments	(31)	(20)		
Received: Tangible fixed assets	76	140		
Trade loans	62	92		
Other fixed asset investments	3	51		
Capital expenditure and financial investment		(615)		(453)
Acquisitions	(417)	(17)		
Cash and overdrafts acquired	1	1		
Disposals	2,290	–		
Cash and overdrafts disposed	(56)	–		
Acquisitions and disposals		1,818		(16)
Equity dividends		(285)		(245)
Net cash flow		1,732		(27)
Management of liquid resources and financing		(1,818)		95
Movement in cash and overdrafts		(86)		68

4.4 NOTES TO THE ACCOUNTS

Key Ideas

Accounting policies

In studying the annual report of a company you will be primarily interested in the statements made by the directors, and the three key financial statements – the **profit and loss account**, the **balance sheet**, and the **cash flow statement**. However, it is worth briefly mentioning the importance of the notes to the accounts.

The notes appear in the back of the report and will usually be set out in considerable detail. The notes refer to the numbered points which are set out in the financial statements.

Accounting policies

The reader of a set of accounts needs to know how they have been constructed. When a company applies a uniform set of accounting policies it is possible to make comparisons between one year and the next and to make comparisons between companies.

For example, the notes for the Annual Report and Accounts for Leicester City plc in 2000 started off by saying:

Accounting policies

Basis of Accounting

The financial statements have been prepared under the **historical cost convention** and in accordance with applicable accounting standards.

Basis of Consolidation

The financial statements are prepared under the historical cost convention and include the results of the parent company and its subsidiary undertakings. The financial statements have been prepared on a **going concern basis**.

Doctor Proctor outlines... NOTES TO THE ACCOUNTS

The notes for Leicester City show the accounting standards that the company is abiding by.

The historical cost convention shows that ... the accounts have been based on the cost incurred **when** an asset was acquired or the amount incurred **when** a liability was created (rather than at higher values resulting from increases in price due to inflation).

- The basis of consolidation shows the business entity that the accounts cover ... in this case the accounts cover the parent company and subsidiary undertakings.

- The going concern basis shows that 'the company will continue in operational existence for the foreseeable future'.

The notes then go on to provide helpful explanations for the reader, for example that:

- turnover represents all income excluding transfer fees and value added tax

- tangible fixed assets are stated at cost

- signing-on fees and loyalty payments are charged to the p&l account over the contract period of each player, etc.

Most company accounts also include a segmental analysis breaking down company activities. For example, P&O Princess Cruises provide a segmental analysis showing aspects such as turnover, profit, capital expenditure, etc. and how this is broken up between its operations in North America, Europe and Australia.

4.4 NOTES TO THE ACCOUNTS

If the company is engaged in more than one type of business, or more than one geographical market, a **segmental analysis** is required, with each business or geographical area being considered as a separate segment. Companies need to analyse the turnover, operating profit and net assets of the business according to relevant business segments.

Leicester City provide a segmental analysis of turnover showing how it is generated. For example, Leicester City use two major headings for turnover – **playing** and **business operations**.

	£000
Playing	
Match receipts	7,967
Television and media related	11,112
	19,079
Business operations	
Retailing and merchandising	1,466
Conference, banqueting and catering	2,422
Sponsorship, executive suites, advertising and other income	3,071
	6,959
	26,038

Other items that will often appear in the notes to the accounts will include:

- profit on the sale of fixed assets
- a breakdown of the net interest payable by the company
- a breakdown showing the ingredients of staff costs
- a statement showing tax paid
- an explanation of dividends paid to shareholders
- an outline and explanation of intangible and tangible fixed assets and depreciation policies
- an outline of the investments made by the company
- breakdowns of the type and nature of debtors and creditors and amounts due and amounts owed
- details of grants
- a detailed breakdown of share capital
- a statement of company reserves
- a statement of the movements in shareholders' funds from the previous year
- an outline of pension arrangements
- a statement setting out liabilities and other commitments
- a notice of the Annual General Meeting of the company and what is to be covered, etc.

You should use these notes to help you get a better understanding of items in the accounts that you do not understand or where further clarification is required.

The notes are very helpful: different businesses set out their accounts differently because of the nature of the business they are in. For example, a manufacturing company will set out its accounts differently to a trading company. In the case of a professional football club a major cost or expense is made up of players' wages. Some clubs include the wages in their cost of sales while others include wages as an expense. The reader of the accounts needs to know where these figures appear – hence the importance of notes.

4.5 REPORTING BUSINESS CHANGES

Key Ideas

Exceptional items

If the company has acquired or terminated business activities, or has experienced some other unusual circumstances, this will need to be highlighted clearly.

When these unusual circumstances occur it is difficult for the reader of the accounts to compare one period with another.

Accounting standards require further information to be included in cases where:

1 The company has acquired new businesses, or sold or terminated previous activities;

2 The company has experienced an exceptional item, i.e. an event or factor that is either unusual in itself, or is of an unusual size or scale.

Where business acquisitions or terminations have taken place, turnover, cost of sales, expenses and operating profit must be analysed between the relevant parts of the business.

Turnover and profit must be analysed in the profit and loss account. The other items are usually analysed in notes to the accounts.

The table below shows how 'unusual circumstances' might appear in a set of accounts.

What does the table tell you about the relative profitability of the business's continuing and discontinued activities? What does it imply for the future?

		£000
Turnover	Continuing operations	5,000
	Acquisitions	2,000
		7,000
	Discontinued operations	500
		7,500
Cost of sales		4,000
Gross profit	(analysed in a supporting note)	3,500
Distribution costs		1,000
Administration expenses		1,000
Operating profit	Continuing operations	1,250
	Acquisitions	500
		1,750
	Discontinued operations	−250
		1,500

4.5 REPORTING BUSINESS CHANGES

Key Ideas 🔑

Exceptional items

The guidelines for reporting exceptional items are explained below.

Dr Proctor says:

'You Must Know This!'

Exceptional items in a company's accounts must be reported in accordance with the rules, or they may give a misleading picture of the business's overall financial performance.

Doctor Proctor outlines... REPORTING EXCEPTIONAL ITEMS

An item is **exceptional** if:

- It does not usually occur, e.g. redundancy payments on closing down a factory;

- It is unusually large, e.g. a major customer defaults on a debt to the company.

Exceptional items are shown in the profit and loss account or are detailed in notes to the accounts.

By extracting the exceptional item it is possible to form a more accurate view of the underlying trend in financial performance.

In the example, analysis shows that profits only increased in 2003 due to the exceptional items. As you can see, this puts a completely different complexion on the company's financial performance.

Example

Manchester United plc reported an exceptional increase in their administrative expenses in their profit and loss account for the six months ended 31 January 2001 as a result of the exceptional costs involved in restructuring their merchandising operations (e.g. the sale of a whole range of Manchester United souvenirs).

	£000
Group turnover	72,008
Cost of sales	(13,184)
Gross profit	58,824
Administrative expenses, before exceptional costs	(37,416)
Administrative expenses – exceptional costs	(739)
Total administrative expenses	(38,155)
Group operating profit	20,669

4.6 THE AUDITOR'S OPINION

Key Ideas 🔑

Consistency

It is essential that accounts are presented in a true and fair way and in line with the accounting principle of consistency. The principle of consistency is concerned with using the same accounting procedures from one year to the next, e.g. in the way in which costs are calculated, in accounting for depreciation, etc.

In the 2000 Annual Report and Accounts for Leicester City, the Auditor Pricewaterhouse Coopers were able to state:

The auditor was thus able to give the opinion that:

Basis of Audit Opinion

'We conducted our audit in accordance with Auditing Standards issued by the Auditing Practices Board. An audit includes examination, on a test basis, of evidence related to the amounts and disclosures in the financial statements. It also includes an assessment of the significant estimates and judgements made by the Directors in the preparation of the financial statements, and of whether the accounting policies are appropriate to the Company's circumstances, consistently applied and adequately disclosed.'

Opinion

'In our opinion the financial statements give a true and fair view of the state of affairs of the Company and the Group at 31 July 2000 and of the profit and cashflows of the Group for the year then ended and have been properly prepared in accordance with the Companies Act 1985.'

4.7 FINANCIAL STATEMENTS SUMMARY

The Profit and Loss Account shows how the profit or loss of a business is arrived at in a particular time period

Notes to Accounts – provide more detailed explanations of numbered notes

The Auditor's Opinion sets out whether the auditor thinks the accounts are true and fair

Remember the main forms of financial statements

The Balance Sheet illustrates the business financial position at a moment in time

The Cash Flow Statement shows inflows and outflows of cash to the business in a given time period

Section 4.1: The Profit and Loss Account

1 The figures below set out an extract from a profit and loss account. Work out the missing figures for
a) gross profit
b) operating profit
c) profit before taxation
d) profit for the financial year (after tax)
e) profit retained.

Profit and Loss Account for Superior Leisure at 31 December 2003

	£m
Turnover	350
Cost of sales	200
Gross profit	?
Administrative expenses	50
Operating profit	?
Interest payable	(10)
Profit before taxation	?
Taxation	(15)
Profit for the financial year (after tax)	?
Dividends	25
Profit retained	?

2 What is meant by a) turnover b) cost of sales and c) expenses?

Section 4.2: The Balance Sheet

1 What is the difference between assets and liabilities?
2 Complete the equation: Assets =
3 Give an example of a tangible fixed asset.
4 Give an example of an intangible fixed asset.
5 Rank the three types of current assets in order of liquidity.
6 What is the working capital of a business? How is it calculated?
7 What is the relationship between the total net assets of a company and capital and reserves?

Section 4.3: The Cash Flow Statement

1 What is typically the main source of cash inflow to a company?
2 Give two other possible sources of cash inflows.
3 Explain three typical sources of cash outflows from a company.

Section 4.4: Notes to the Accounts

1 What is meant by historical cost?
2 What sort of information will be set out in a segmental analysis?
3 Identify one other piece of information that might appear in the notes to the accounts.

Section 4.5: Reporting Business Changes

1 Give two examples of exceptional items that might appear in a profit and loss account.
2 Why is it important to account for exceptional items?

Section 4.6: The Auditor's Opinion

1 What is the role of the auditor?
2 Why is it important for the auditor to report that accounting standards have been consistent within a company?

Topics covered in this unit

5.1 Introduction to Ratio Analysis

How to calculate an accounting ratio and extract ratios from the profit and loss account and balance sheet.

5.2 Profitability Ratios

How to calculate and then analyse profit margins.

5.3 Liquidity Ratios

How to check whether a business has sufficient (or even too many) liquid assets.

5.4 Return on Capital Ratios

How to compare sales with the financial resources of a business.

5.5 Gearing Ratios

How to examine company accounts in terms of the relationship between owners' capital and the capital provided by long-term loans and preference shares.

5.6 Efficiency Ratios

How to examine how well a business is using its assets, usually in the generation of sales.

5.7 Limitations of Ratio Analysis

Why ratio analysis doesn't give us the full picture.

Questions

This unit shows you how to use and apply various ratios which will help you to analyse the performance of a company. The material here is largely based on the profit and loss account on page 50 and the balance sheet on page 51.

5.1 INTRODUCTION TO RATIO ANALYSIS

For illustrative purposes, Unit 5 of this book is based on data from the financial statements shown on this page and the next one for a fictional leisure company – Better Leisure plc.

The values stated in the financial statements of a business have more meaning if they are analysed in relative terms. As you can see in the statements below, we compare 2002 with 2001.

Better Leisure plc
Profit and Loss Account for 2002

	2002 £000	2001 £000	
Turnover	90,000	60,000	
Cost of sales	60,000	40,000	
Gross profit	30,000	20,000	
Administrative expenses	15,000	10,000	
Operating profit	15,000	10,000	
Interest paid	1,500	1,000	
Profit before taxation	13,500	9,000	
Corporation tax	3,500	2,500	
Profit after taxation	10,000	6,500	
Dividends	2,500	1,500	
Retained profit for the year	7,500	5,000	

Better Leisure plc

5.1 INTRODUCTION TO RATIO ANALYSIS

Better Leisure plc
Balance Sheet

	2002 £000	2001 £000
Fixed assets	200,000	125,000
Current assets:		
Stocks	2,500	2,000
Debtors	15,000	10,000
Cash	7,500	3,000
	25,000	15,000
Creditors due within one year	15,000	10,000
Net current assets	10,000	5,000
Total assets *less* current liabilities	210,000	130,000
Creditors due after one year	60,000	50,000
Net assets	150,000	80,000
Share capital and reserves		
Called up share capital	5,000	4,000
Share premium account	85,000	51,000
Profit and loss account	60,000	25,000
	150,000	80,000

Notes to the accounts

Creditors due within one year

	2002	2001
Bank overdraft	1,000	1,000
Finance lease	5,000	4,000
Trade creditors	4,000	2,000
Other creditors including taxation	5,000	3,000
Total	15,000	10,000

Creditors due after one year

	2002	2001
Loan stock	40,000	30,000
Finance lease	20,000	20,000
Total	60,000	50,000

5.1 INTRODUCTION TO RATIO ANALYSIS

An **accounting ratio** is a comparison of two items from the financial statements of a business:

$$\text{Ratio} = \frac{\text{Value 1}}{\text{Value 2}}$$

Financial ratios are typically taken from the profit and loss and/or balance sheet.

Make sure when you examine a ratio comparing a figure from the profit and loss with the balance sheet that the figure from the profit and loss account is an annual amount.

Methods of ratio analysis

Using values from the balance sheet

Ratios based on two values taken from the balance sheet can tell us a great deal about the capital structure of the business and how financial resources have been used.

Example

Comparing current assets with current liabilities gives you the working capital ratio – showing the extent to which the business has liquid capital to finance day-to-day activities.

Using ratios from the profit and loss account

Ratios based on values taken from the profit and loss account can provide useful information about profitability and reasons for changes in it.

Example

Comparing operating profit with the value of sales (turnover) gives us a good indicator of how effectively a business is generating profits from its sales.

Using ratios from the balance sheet and the profit and loss account

Ratios that are based on one value from the profit and loss account and one from the balance sheet can also give us useful information about the business's financial efficiency.

Example

Comparing the value of debtors to the value of sales shows what period of sales remain unpaid. It therefore tells us how well customer credit is being managed.

5.1 INTRODUCTION TO RATIO ANALYSIS

Doctor Proctor outlines... RATIOS AND BENCHMARKS

Looking at raw accounting ratios makes little sense unless we have something meaningful to compare these figures to.

Effective analysis is therefore only possible if a ratio is compared to a benchmark.

A benchmark may be:

- the same ratio calculated for a different period, such as the previous year. This will provide information about trends.

- the same ratio calculated for comparable businesses. This will provide a means of comparing the financial performance of different companies.

Ratios may be calculated for business units within the same company, such as individual shops within a retail chain, or for similar firms trading during the same period.

A benchmark makes it possible to identify what is achievable by the most successful business or by similar businesses in the same industry.

Other Premier League football teams may set Manchester United profit figures as the benchmark to be achieved.

Manchester United may use their 2002 profits as the benchmark for their 2003 profits.

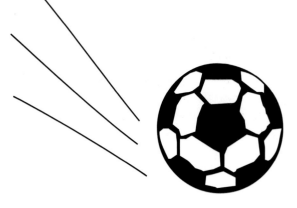

5.2 Profitability Ratios

Key Ideas 🔑

Measuring profitability

Profitability ratios generally take values in the profit and loss account and express them as a percentage of sales revenues.

Profit is an indication of the business's competitive position, both in respect of customers and suppliers. The ideal position is for profits to be high in relation to sales, and for competitive pressures to be weak.

Doctor Proctor Calculates

$$\text{Profit margin} = \frac{\text{Operating profit}}{\text{Sales}} \times 100\%$$

To assess the strength of your profitability ratios you need to compare them with those of similar firms or with your own firm in previous time periods.

Example

The following figures are available for Better Leisure in 2002.

$$\text{Profit margin} = \frac{15,000,000}{90,000,000} \times 100\% = 16.66\%$$

This would be considered a high profit margin, as many firms achieve margins of less than 10%. To assess whether Better Leisure had done well we would need to look at previous years and typical profit margins in the industry.

Activity

Which of these two companies had the higher profit margin in 2000?

	Fitness First plc	Holmes Place plc
	£000	£000
Turnover	52,234	87,699
Operating profit	13,036	15,896

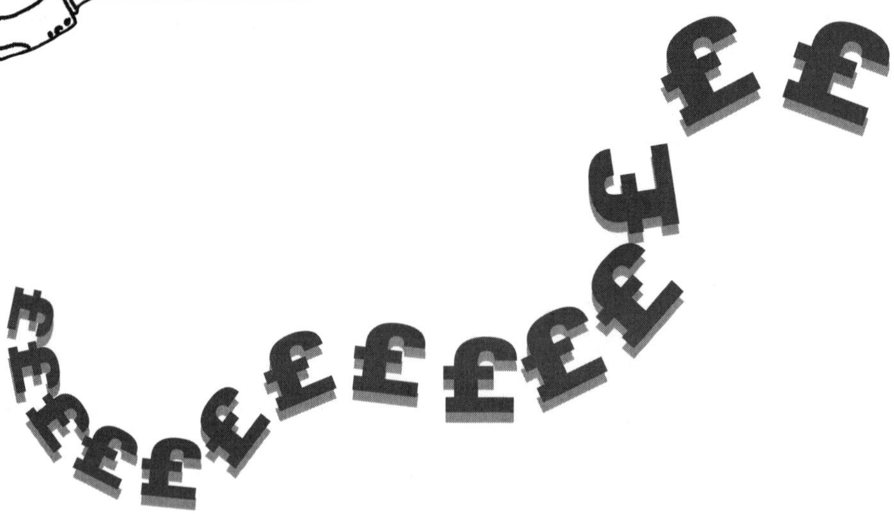

5.2 PROFITABILITY RATIOS

Key Ideas 🔑

Profit margin analysis

It is helpful to analyse profit margins in more detail using cost figures to find out the effects of different types of costs, e.g. wages, administration, etc. on profits. This analysis can reveal that some costs are eating into profits and therefore they need to be controlled more effectively. For example, an important calculation is wages to sales:

$$\textbf{Wages to sales} = \frac{\text{Wages}}{\text{Sales}} \times 100\%$$

We can then check to see if wage rises are holding back profits.

Activity

For Better Leisure plc, in 2002 the following figures are available (see profit and loss account, page 50).

$$\textbf{Ratio of Cost of Sales to Sales} = \frac{\pounds 60{,}000}{\pounds 90{,}000} \times 100\% = 66.6\%$$

$$\textbf{Ratio of Administration Costs to Sales} = \frac{\pounds 15{,}000}{\pounds 90{,}000} \times 100\% = 16.66\%$$

By analysing the business's cost structure and comparing it with other businesses, it is possible to determine the efficiency of various parts of the firm.

For Better Leisure in 2001, calculate the following ratios for 2001 (see profit and loss account, page 50):

a)   Cost of sales to sales.

b)   Administration costs to sales.

Now compare these ratios with those for 2002.

What conclusions can you draw?

5.3 LIQUIDITY RATIOS

Key Ideas 🔑
Defining liquidity

Dr Proctor says:
'You Must Know This!'

Remember that however profitable a business may be, it must always have enough working capital to provide the liquidity to pay its suppliers and employees on a day-to-day basis.

Liquidity is the ease with which an asset can be converted into cash. It is important for a business to have liquid assets to carry out day-to-day spending transactions. Working capital is the liquidity which a business has available at any time to carry out day-to-day trading.

Working capital is measured by **current assets** minus **current liabilities**.

Doctor Proctor outlines... CURRENT RATIO AND ACID TEST RATIO

Two ratios that are commonly used to measure financial liquidity are the current ratio and the more stringent acid test ratio.

The current ratio compares current assets to short-term creditors (who need to be paid back in the immediate future).

Doctor Proctor Calculates

$$\text{Current ratio} = \frac{\text{Current assets}}{\text{Creditors due in less than one year}}$$

The acid test ratio compares only cash and other monetary assets to short-term creditors.

$$\text{Acid test ratio} = \frac{\text{Current assets} - \text{Stock}}{\text{Creditors due in less than one year}}$$

The following figures are available for Better Leisure plc for 2002:

$$\text{Current ratio} = \frac{25,000}{15,000} = 1.66$$

$$\text{Acid test ratio} = \frac{22,500}{15,000} = 1.5$$

Now compare the ratios with 2001.

What conclusions can be drawn?

5.3 LIQUIDITY RATIOS

Key Ideas 🔑

Using liquidity ratios

The higher a business's liquidity ratio, the more assets are available to pay the firm's creditors.

But high ratios may indicate that excessive funds are being tied up in working capital, thus reducing return on capital employed.

Monitoring change

A change in the ratios may be due to a change in assets or a change in liabilities. It is important to know the exact cause, because this will determine whether the change is for the better or for the worse.

For example, a reduction in the current ratio could be caused by either a reduction in stocks due to improved stock control (a change for the better) or an increase in liabilities (a change for the worse).

What is an ideal liquidity ratio?

It is difficult to generalise about the size of the ideal liquidity ratio because it varies so much with the type of business concerned. For example, a large retail chain may be able to get away with low liquidity ratios because it buys goods on credit, and will often receive the money from the customer even before they have received invoices from suppliers. In contrast a manufacturing company may need more liquidity because of the time required to receive payment from goods sold on credit. You may read that a current ratio of 2.0 and an acid test ratio of 1.0 are 'ideal' benchmarks – but it all depends on the situation.

Activity

Work out the current and acid test ratios for Sunderland plc for 2001.

As at 31 July 2001

	£000
Current assets	
Stocks	191
Debtors	9,112
Short-term deposits	1,405
Cash at bank and in hand	1,008
	11,716
Creditors (amounts falling due within one year)	(32,700)

Why might Premier League football clubs be able to sustain the sort of ratio outlined above?

5.4 RETURN ON CAPITAL RATIOS

Key Ideas 🔑

Calculating financial return

Ratios that compare profit with capital invested are an extremely useful way of measuring financial return. They allow investors to compare different companies' performance and choose the most profitable investment opportunity.

Return on equity

Just as private individuals expect a reasonable return on their savings (e.g. in a Building Society or Bank), shareholders expect a certain minimum return on their investment. Return on equity measures the return on equity capital. This will be higher in some businesses and industries than in others.

Dr Proctor says:
'You Must Know This!'

The term used to describe the financial return that investors expect is called the **Cost of Capital**. Return on Equity shows us whether a company is covering the cost of capital. Company directors are responsible to their shareholders, so achieving a satisfactory return on equity is a key measure of how well they are doing.

Doctor Proctor Calculates

$$\text{Return on equity} = \frac{\text{Profit (after tax and preference share dividends)}}{\text{Ordinary share capital and reserves}}$$

Activity

The following figures are available for Better Leisure plc for 2002 (see accounts on pages 50–51)

$$\text{Return on equity} = \frac{10,000}{1,500,000} \times 100\% = 6.66\%$$

Calculate the return on equity for 2001.

Assuming that shareholders expect a return of 7 per cent, what do the figures show?

5.4 RETURN ON CAPITAL RATIOS

Key Ideas

Return on capital employed (ROCE)

ROCE measures the return on all forms of capital employed in a business (not just shareholders' capital).

$$\text{ROCE} = \frac{\text{Operating profit}}{\text{Total capital employed}} \times 100\%$$

In terms of managing the running of a company this is the most important indicator of financial performance. This is because companies usually raise finance from a number of different sources e.g. loans, overdrafts etc. It is necessary for total profits to cover the **total cost** of capital, including debt finance.

Doctor Proctor outlines...
OPERATING PROFIT AND CAPITAL EMPLOYED

Operating profit is calculated **after** deducting expenses, but **before** deducting interest payments.

Total capital employed can be calculated in two ways, both of which produce the same result:

1 The 'net asset' approach:

    Fixed assets
  + Stock
  + Debtors
  − Creditors (non-financing)

2 The 'sources of finance' approach:

    Share capital and reserves
  + Finance creditors
    (including loans, overdrafts, HP and leases)
  − Cash

Activity

Using the 'net asset' approach, Better Leisure plc's capital employed for 2002 is calculated as follows:

	£000
Fixed assets	200,000
Stocks	2,500
Debtors	15,000
Less trade creditors	4,000
Other creditors	5,000
	208,500

Using the 'sources of finance' approach, Better Leisure plc's capital employed for 2002 is calculated as follows:

	£000
Share capital	150,000
Bank overdraft	1,000
Finance lease	25,000
Loan stock	40,000
Less cash	7,500
	208,500

$$\text{ROCE} = \frac{15{,}000{,}000}{208{,}500{,}000} = 7.19\%$$

Using figures from page 51, calculate the 'return on capital employed' for 2001.

What can be deduced from these ratios?

It is also important to remember that interest on these other forms of capital must be paid back before ordinary shareholders can receive dividends.

5.5 GEARING RATIOS

What is gearing?

Gearing is the term used to describe the relationship between finance that receives a fixed rate of return and equity (capital that receives profit-related returns).

Fixed return finance consists of preference shares and net debt, where net debt is made up of all interest-bearing finance (such as loans and leases) less cash holdings. The equity of a company includes ordinary share capital, retained earnings and other reserves.

Gearing describes the relationship between finance that enjoys a fixed rate of return, irrespective of how much profit the business makes, and equity that enjoys profit-related returns.

The **gearing ratio** indicates the proportion of capital contributed by the real owners of the company – the ordinary shareholders. If shareholders have contributed too little capital, there is a danger that the company may have to pay crippling interest payments.

Doctor Proctor Calculates

$$\text{Gearing ratio} = \frac{\text{Net debt} + \text{Preference shares}}{\text{Ordinary share capital}}$$

Doctor Proctor outlines... GEARING AND INVESTMENT RISK

The gearing structure of a company affects the return to investors and the risks involved.

In general, the more risky an investment the higher the returns that investors expect to make.

Fixed interest investors, e.g. preference shareholders, are paid first and therefore have to accept a modest fixed return on their investment.

Ordinary shareholders receive the profits that are left over (some years this will be a good return, other years not so good).

More fixed interest finance raised by the company will lead to greater interest payments that will

need to be paid before the ordinary shareholders get their share. Thus the more fixed interest borrowing that the company makes, the bigger the risk for the ordinary shareholder.

As total profits change, the effect on the residual amount (what is left for ordinary shareholders after paying a fixed amount of interest) will be proportionately greater – the **gearing effect**.

For shareholders, gearing will be beneficial if return on capital employed is higher than interest on loans – but it can be catastrophic if the business hits lean times.

5.5 GEARING RATIOS

Let me show you how gearing can make ordinary shareholder returns more volatile.

Example

Three companies employ £100,000 of capital each.

In any one year they can generate profits in the range of £5,000–£20,000 before deducting interest on debt. Each company is financed by a different mixture of ordinary shares and debentures.

Finance

	Shares	Debentures	Gearing ratio
Company A	£10,000	£90,000	£90,000/£10,000 = 9
Company B	£50,000	£50,000	£50,000/£50,000 = 1
Company C	£90,000	£10,000	£10,000/£90,000 = 0.11

The table below shows how differing gearing levels affect profit levels:

Company	A	B	C
Capital structure			
Ordinary shares	10,000	50,000	90,000
Debentures at 10% p.a.	90,000	50,000	10,000
	100,000	100,000	100,000
Allocation of profits of £5,000			
Ordinary shares	-4,000	0	4,000
Debentures 10%	9,000	5,000	1,000
	5,000	5,000	5,000
Allocation of profits of £10,000			
Ordinary shares	1,000	5,000	9,000
Debentures 10%	9,000	5,000	1,000
	10,000	10,000	10,000
Allocation of profits of £20,000			
Ordinary shares	11,000	15,000	19,000
Debentures 10%	9,000	5,000	1,000
	20,000	20,000	20,000

Whatever the level of profits, debenture-holders will always receive 10 per cent of the value of debentures, e.g. £9,000 when £90,000 of debentures have been issued. However, the percentage returns enjoyed by ordinary shareholders varies widely, being dependent on gearing in addition to the level of profits.

5.5 GEARING RATIOS

> **Example**
>
> Taking the nine scenarios from the previous page, the percentage returns to ordinary shareholders are:
>
> | Company | A | B | C |
> |---|---|---|---|
> | Gearing | 9 | 1 | 0.11 |
> | | More risky: possible high profits or heavy losses. | | More certainty of a modest return. |
> | On profits of £5,000 | −40% | 0% | 4.4% |
> | On profits of £10,000 | 10% | 10% | 10% |
> | On profits of £20,000 | 110% | 30% | 21.1% |
> | Range of returns | 150% | 30% | 16.7% |
>
> In general, ratios under 0.25 indicate low gearing and values in excess of 1 show high gearing.

Interest cover

Another valuable measure of financial risk is the relationship of interest payments to the profits generated by the business.

This is known as **interest cover**. The larger the interest cover, the less risk in the future of interest payments pushing the business into a loss.

> **Doctor Proctor Calculates**
>
> $$\text{Interest cover} = \frac{\text{Profit before interest}}{\text{Interest paid}}$$

> **Activity**
>
> Using the figures above for Companies A, B and C, the following interest cover ratios can be calculated when profit before interest is £10,000:
>
> | | | Interest cover |
> |---|---|---|
> | Company A $= \dfrac{£10,000}{£9,000} =$ | | 1.11 |
> | Company B $= \dfrac{£10,000}{£5,000} =$ | | 2 |
> | Company C $= \dfrac{£10,000}{£1,000} =$ | | 10 |
>
> Calculate the gearing ratio and interest cover for Better Leisure plc for 2002 and 2001.
>
> Evaluate the figures. What conclusion can you draw?

5.6 EFFICIENCY RATIOS

Key Ideas 🔑

What is an efficiency ratio?

An efficient asset

Efficiency ratios are a measure of how well a business organisation is using its assets. The assets used by a business generate sales – the more sales they generate the more efficient those assets are. For example, a football player like Ruud Van Niestelroy, the Manchester United striker, is able to generate lots of extra sales for the club by enabling Manchester United to sell more shirts and other souvenirs.

Efficiency ratios measure the volume of business activity relative to the amount invested in the relevant assets of the business.

Doctor Proctor Calculates

$$\text{Efficiency ratio} = \frac{\text{Volume or value of transactions}}{\text{Value of assets}}$$

Efficiency ratios are concerned with the amount of sales relative to the financial resources invested in the business.

The more capital that is tied up in a business, the greater the level of sales that need to be generated to be efficient.

A football club that does not attract many supporters through the turnstiles is unlikely to generate much profit for its owners!

Doctor Proctor Calculates

Like other ratios, efficiency ratios can be benchmarked against past performance and against the performance of other businesses in the same industry.

If efficiency remains constant, then any increase in investment should result in a proportionate increase in output.

In theory, efficiency ratios should be as high as possible – although in many cases there is a trade-off between volume and prices, which may affect profitability.

Learn the formulas for the following efficiency ratios:

Utilisation of capital employed $= \dfrac{\text{Sales}}{\text{Capital employed}}$

Utilisation of fixed assets $= \dfrac{\text{Sales}}{\text{Fixed assets}}$

Utilisation of current assets $= \dfrac{\text{Sales}}{\text{Current assets}}$

5.6 EFFICIENCY RATIOS

Key Ideas

Other efficiency ratios

A number of other ratios are helpful for measuring the efficiency with which different types of assets are used.

The following examples are based on figures taken from the profit and loss account and balance sheet for a supermarket chain.

	£000	
Sales (turnover)	90,000	(p&l account)
Cost of sales	60,000	(p&l account)
Stock	1,000	(balance sheet)
Debtors	100	(balance sheet)
Trade creditors	5000	(notes)

Stock turnover, as the name suggests, measures how many times the stock is turned over in a given period (e.g. one year). Typical levels of stock turnover vary from business to business – e.g. supermarkets have much higher stock turnovers than antique shops.

Doctor Proctor Calculates

$$\text{Stock turnover} = \frac{\text{Cost of sales}}{\text{Stock}}$$

Using figures for the supermarket chain, stock turnover in 2002 is:

$$\frac{60,000,000}{1,000,000} = 60$$

This indicates a high level of stock turnover with stock being replenished 60 times a year. Of course, some stock (e.g. milk) would be replaced almost every day of the week, whereas other items (e.g. videos) might take several weeks to sell. High stock turnover indicates good stock control.

Debtor days are a measure of the average number of days it takes debtors to pay up. A low number of debtor days indicates good credit control. Comparisons should be made for the same firm in previous time periods and with other firms in the same line of business.

Doctor Proctor Calculates

$$\text{Debtor days} = \frac{\text{Debtors}}{\text{Credit sales}} \times 365 \text{ days}$$

(number of days in the year)

In the example given for our retail chain,

$$\text{Debtor days} = \frac{100,000 \times 365}{900,000,000} = 0.04 \text{ days}$$

Typically, supermarkets don't trade on a credit basis except in areas such as dry cleaning, so debtor days are almost non existent.

Creditor days show on average how long a business takes to pay its suppliers.

Doctor Proctor Calculates

$$\text{Creditor days} = \frac{\text{Trade creditors}}{\text{Cost of sales}} \times 365 \text{ days}$$

For the supermarket chain:

$$\text{Creditor days} = \frac{5,000,000 \times 365}{60,000,000} = 30.4 \text{ days}$$

The ratio shows that the supermarket chain takes on average 30.4 days to pay its suppliers.

Whilst a high ratio is good for cash flow (it is better to have cash in your own bank account rather than someone else's), it can also be an indication of cash flow problems and poor relations with suppliers.

5.7 LIMITATIONS OF RATIO ANALYSIS

Key Ideas 🔑

Drawbacks to ratio analysis

While ratio analysis is a powerful tool, it has its drawbacks. Here are some weaknesses.

1 Financial performance indicators place emphasis on short-term results. As a result, businesses may seek to maximise short-term gains at the expense of the long-term growth of the company.

2 The external financial analyst has to use information that is at least several months old.

3 In order for ratio analysis to be carried out in full, published accounts must provide enough detail to work on. Often there is important information missing.

4 Comparison of ratios between companies is difficult, as the business activities of different firms are rarely identical.

5 Some values may be affected more than others by changes in price levels. In particular, the value of property used in the business will depend very much on when it was purchased. Low property valuations will result in artificially high returns on capital employed.

Section 5.1: Introduction to Ratio Analysis

1 What is a financial ratio?
2 Why is it important to compare financial ratios with benchmarks?
3 What sort of benchmarks are appropriate?

Section 5.2: Profitability Ratios

The following figures show the five year record for a well-known construction company:

	1998	1999	2000	2001	2002
Turnover (£m)	659	719	791	840	796
Operating profit (£m)	22	32	47	60	43

1 What has happened to profit margins over the period in question?
2 What factors might have contributed to the change in profit margin over the period shown?
3 How might an analysis of components of the profit margin give a better indication of why the profit margin has altered over the period shown?

Section 5.3: Liquidity Ratios

The following figures are extracted from the Bass (brewing, hotels and resorts) annual report published in September 2000. Figures are taken from the balance sheet.

	2000
Current assets	
Stocks	97
Debtors	600
Investments	826
Cash at bank and in hand	125
	?
Creditors: amounts falling due within one year	(1,604)
Net current assets/(liabilities)	?

1 Why is the figure for creditors shown in brackets?
2 Why is it important for Bass to have working capital?

3 What is the current ratio?
4 What is the acid test ratio?

Section 5.4: Return on Capital Ratios

1 What is meant by the term 'cost of capital'?
2 Why does return on equity need to be higher than the cost of capital?
3 What is the difference between return on equity and return on capital employed?

Section 5.5: Gearing Ratios

Two companies employ exactly the same value of capital. However, while the Green company's capital is made up of 75 per cent fixed interest securities, the Yellow company has raised 75 per cent of its capital from equity.

Assuming that the two companies have similar profit records:

1 In which company are the shareholders taking the biggest risk? Explain why.
2 What is the danger if the Green company continues to sell more preference shares, and to raise capital using loans?
3 What is the gearing in the two companies at the start of the period under consideration?

Section 5.6: Efficiency Ratios

In analysing the annual report of a public company the following information comes to light:

	2001	2002
Debtor days	50	65
Creditor days	50	50
Stock turnover	15	10
Utilisation of capital employed	1.5	1.2

1 Show how each of these ratios would be calculated.
2 Which of these ratios would be a cause for concern? Why?

Section 5.7: Limitations of Ratio Analysis

Explain two reasons why it is important to be cautious when using ratios to analyse the performance of businesses.

Topics covered in this unit

This unit examines key features of media presentation of financial information about company shares and bonds including information presented in newspapers, in television reports, the radio, the Internet, etc. It focuses particularly on newspaper reporting.

6.1 Reading the Financial Pages of a Newspaper

An introduction to the sorts of information that appear in the financial pages of a newspaper coupled with an introduction to equities, i.e. ordinary shares.

6.2 Buying and Selling Equities

Outlines the role of the Stock Exchange and Stock Exchange dealing as the market for the shares of public companies. Explains how share prices and other details of interest to investors are presented in newspaper reports.

6.3 Important Ratios for Shareholders

Examines the key ratios that investors will examine in weighing up the prospects of alternative shares. Also examines other details about share trading which are normally presented in the financial press.

6.4 FTSE and Other Indexes

Explains how share price indexes are calculated and then outlines the importance of FTSE-100 and other share price indexes, used both in the UK and overseas. Shows how these indexes can vary over time depending on whether there is a 'bull' or 'bear' market.

6.5 Company and Government Bonds

Examines the market for fixed interest securities and shows how the price of bonds varies with the prevailing market rate of interest, and the time taken before repayment takes place.

6.6 Managed Fund Prices

Shows how the prices and changes in price of unit trusts are presented in the financial press.

Questions

6.1 READING THE FINANCIAL PAGES OF A NEWSPAPER

Key Ideas 🔑

Equity prices

FINANCIAL TIMES

FTSE 100 plunges below 4,000

You have probably looked at the financial pages of a newspaper and skipped over them because they look incomprehensible. What do they mean?

These pages are made up of a number of sections including:

- equity prices
- prices of company and government bonds
- exchange rates for currencies
- prices of metals, agricultural products and other commodities
- energy prices
- money market prices and bond yields.

It is important to develop a broad understanding of the various financial products which are being traded on various organised markets.

This unit examines share and bond prices. The following unit introduces a range of other financial information that is presented in the media.

Introduction to equities

Pride of place is given in newspaper financial coverage to the reporting of details about companies, their share price and current performance.

Example

A typical example of newspaper reporting for a building company would be presented as follows:

Superior Builders						
(Market value of shares £449m, current share price 419p)						
Five-year record	**1998**	**1999**	**2000**	**2001**	**2002**	**(year ended 31.12)**
Turnover (£m)	659	719	791	840	796	Value of sales in each year
Pre-tax profits (£m)	22.3	32.5	46.6	60.0	42.5	Profits
Earnings per share (p)	18.3	20.8	30.9	40.2	29.8	Profit divided by number of shares
Dividend per share (p)	7.50	8.00	8.80	10.0	10.0	Dividend paid on each share

6.1 READING THE FINANCIAL PAGES OF A NEWSPAPER

The chart below indicates changes in share price. Share prices rose considerably because of the high levels of profits achieved in 2000 and 2001 and because the company report and other financial information showed that the company was gaining a larger share of the market nationally as well as expanding into lucrative overseas markets.

Superior Builders share price

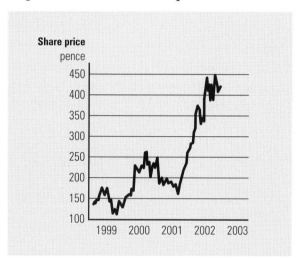

The term **stock** refers to the stock of capital money belonging to a company; shareholders are people with a share in this stock. The share price is determined by the intensity of demand for particular types of shares. If a lot of people want to buy shares in a company this will push its share price up.

Doctor Proctor outlines... RETURNS ON SHARES

The returns for preference shareholders and loan stockholders tend to be explicit. For example, a loan stock contract might be phrased like this:

'Loan stock 8%, August 2008. Will pay the holder £8 per annum for every £100 of stock owned until redemption in 2008 ...'

The situation for ordinary shareholders is less clear. The return they receive depends on the profitability of the business, and this may be volatile over time.

Ordinary shareholders can benefit from holding shares in a number of ways:

1   The value of their shares grow over time as prices rise. This will be the case in companies which are successful and where investors have confidence.

2   They receive yield/return in the form of dividends on shares. Profitable companies will be best placed to pay good dividends.

3   They are a part owner of a company and have the right to elect directors and to vote on key issues at an Annual General Meeting.

4   They have the option to buy additional shares at a favourable price (rights issue).

5   They have the right to reductions in prices of company products, e.g. subsidised ferry travel in the case of Channel Ferry companies, etc.

6.2 BUYING AND SELLING EQUITIES

Key Ideas

The Stock Exchange

The London Stock Exchange provides a market for companies wanting to issue shares for the first time as well as for the trading of existing shares and other securities.

Ordinary shares in companies are traded on the **London Stock Exchange**. The LSE trades both UK shares and large volumes of international equities using an electronic price quotation system called **SEAQ International**. Companies whose shares are listed on the Stock Exchange can have their shares traded using this system.

The **Alternative Investment Market (AIM)** is also run by the Stock Exchange. Typically, AIM companies are smaller and younger ones who will often progress to a full listing at a later stage. It is cheaper for companies to be listed on the AIM because there are fewer listing requirements.

Buying and selling shares in this country is dominated by the large financial institutions such as pension funds and insurance companies (over half of all shares). Foreign investors own about a quarter of all shares.

Private investors therefore only own about 17 per cent of all shares, and about half of these only have shares in one or two companies.

To buy or sell shares an individual will normally get someone (a broker) to trade shares on their behalf e.g. their bank or an Internet-based share trading company. They will have to pay a commission for this service, which tends to be expensive for small deals.

Doctor Proctor outlines... ROLE OF MARKETMAKING

Marketmakers are firms trading through the Stock Exchange that today are usually owned by banks and other financial institutions.

The marketmaker has a responsibility to guarantee a market in particular types of shares so they must keep stocks of these shares on their books – e.g. creating a market in oil shares.

The marketmaker makes a profit from what is called a **spread** – i.e. the difference between the price at which they sell (the offered price) and the price at which they buy shares (the bid price).

e.g.	Offered price	102p
	Bid price	100p
	Spread =	2p

6.2 BUYING AND SELLING EQUITIES

The share trading dealer will buy or sell shares through marketmakers at the Stock Exchange.

In theory prices are very competitive because marketmakers compete against each other with their prices being listed on the SEAQ screens.

If you decide to buy 1000 Marks and Spencer shares your share dealer will buy these on your behalf at the best market price available. The shares will then be paid for several days later on the **Settlement Day**.

Today, the process of share dealing has been simplified through the **Stock Exchange Electronic Trading Service (SETS)**. This is a computer based system designed to match buyers and sellers of shares, reducing the need for the middleman. Whereas the SEAQ system just gave information on prices, the SETS system can carry out trades. For example, if a seller wants to sell 100,000 Marks and Spencer shares and at the same time a buyer wants to buy 100,000 shares the deal can be matched up over the SETS system rather than going through a marketmaker.

Doctor Proctor outlines... THE STOCK EXCHANGE SHARE PRICE LIST

Here is an extract from the Stock Exchange share price list in the Leisure, Entertainment and Hotels section of a national newspaper for Thursday 17 January 2002. Note that the share prices relate to the previous day:

Leisure, Entertainment and Hotels

52 weeks						
High	Low	Stock	Price	Change	Yield	P/E
336	110	Airtours	258.2	2.2	3.7	27.8
571	398	**Compass**	512.0	5.0	1.1	25.6
355	234	De Vere	310.0	−8.0	3.4	12.1
74	35	Domino's Pizza	72.5	0.0	1.4	24.7
256	162	**Hilton**	223.5	−7.2	3.9	15.8
227	118	Manchester United	144.5	0.5	1.4	24.8
411	180	**P&O Princess**	411.0	4.5	3.1	15.8

6.2 BUYING AND SELLING EQUITIES

Equity prices

Typically, equity prices will be presented in a full page of a broadsheet newspaper. The shares are presented sector by sector in an alphabetical listing, for example:

> Aerospace and Defence
> Automobiles
> Banks
> Beverages
> Chemicals
> Construction and Building
> Etc.

Listed shares are presented under each of these headings. Companies marked in bold type make up the Financial Times – Stock Exchange 100 Index (FTSE 100) of top British companies. The FTSE 100 Index shows what is happening to the average price of these 100 companies.

In the extract on page 71 the first two columns set out the highest and lowest prices the shares have been in the previous twelve months. The stock name is listed, as is its average price on the day before the paper was published. The change shows the price change between 15 and 16 January.

The first things to note about the prices listed above are that:

- Compass, Hilton and P&O Princess are all FTSE 100 listed companies, indicating that these are well established companies.

- Most of the shares are somewhat below their high for the year; for example, Airtours share price was at its highest at 336 pence – on 17 January it was only 258.2 pence. It is not surprising that a travel business should suffer as a result of the loss of confidence in flying following the events of 11 September 2001. As expected, the whole sector was suffering: P&O Princess is the only company at its high for the year as a result of take-over activity.

- The prices of Airtours, Compass, Manchester United and P&O Princess have all risen on the previous day, as shown by the change column. Domino's Pizza share price has remained constant. Hilton and De Vere hotel prices have both fallen.

Share prices are quoted in pence and fractions of pence, unless otherwise stated. The price listed for each share is the middle price, which is halfway between the price the share is offered at by the sellers and the price it is bid for by the buyer.

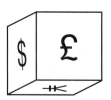
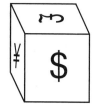
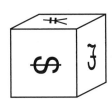

6.3 IMPORTANT RATIOS FOR SHAREHOLDERS

Key Ideas

Calculating the return on shares

Investors buy equities principally because they expect the value of shares to increase. Over a long period of time share prices increase when the earning power of the company increases, so that they are able to pay higher dividends.

Investors need information about the returns on different types of shares. For example, they may want to compare the returns on ordinary shares, preference shares or loan stock.

Doctor Proctor Calculates

Here's an easy way to calculate returns on ordinary shares.

$$\text{Total ordinary shareholder's return} = \frac{(\text{Dividend} + \text{change in share price})}{\text{Share price}} \times 100\%$$

Of course, it's easy to measure the return on shares after the event, but investors want to know the likelihood of a good return before they make their investment!

Doctor Proctor Calculates

One way to evaluate a company's shares is to consider the amount of profit generated for every share in issue – this is called the earnings per share approach. This is calculated as follows:

Earnings per share (EPS)

$$= \frac{\text{Net Profit (after tax and preference dividend)}}{\text{Average number of ordinary shares in issue}}$$

The figures for earnings per share of a company are presented in the company report at the foot of the profit and loss account. There will also be an accompanying note to show how these earnings are calculated.

Example

For example, for Bettertours (a package tour company) the following information was provided for 2002.

Net profit (earnings)	£10,165,000
Shares in 2002	46,904,000

Therefore the earnings per share was 21.7 pence.

This is a valuable measure, because individual shareholders clearly want to know how much profit their shares have earned. But if the company issues more shares, its profits will have to be shared out over a wider capital base. Shareholders therefore want to know that the EPS will be maintained and, if possible, increased. This can only be achieved if the company makes a profit.

6.3 IMPORTANT RATIOS FOR SHAREHOLDERS

> **Key Ideas**
>
> **Dividend yield and price/earnings ratio**

A second approach to measuring ordinary shareholders' returns is to look at the actual cash dividend paid each year. Dividends are different from profits earned because many firms retain some funds to finance future growth or to replace debt. The **dividend** is the share of profit that the shareholders receive (the rest being retained).

> A particularly useful way to measure share performance is to compare earnings per share with the share price.
>
> The **price/earnings ratio** shows how many years it will take for current earnings to pay for a share in the company.

Doctor Proctor Calculates

$$\text{Dividend Yield} = \frac{\text{Dividend per share}}{\text{Share price}} \times 100\%$$

Example

Assume that the share price of Bettertours is £5 and out of its £10,165,000 profit Bettertours decides to retain £8,165,000 in the business – then the dividend per share in 2002 is:

$$\frac{£2,000,000}{46,904,000} = 4.3 \text{ pence}$$

Dividend yield is therefore:

$$\frac{£0.43 \times 100\%}{£5.0} = 8.6\%$$

This provides a good return to the investor which can then be coupled with appreciations in the price of the share.

The variations in price/earnings ratios reflect investors' different views about the growth potential of the companies concerned. If investors are confident they will bid up the price of shares so that the share price rapidly increases as a multiple of earnings.

If the outlook for growth is good, a company will command a high P/E ratio (anything from 20 upwards).

A ratio of under 10 indicates doubts over growth – at least in the short term.

> **Activity**
>
> Look at the table below showing the Yield and P/E ratio of firms in the Leisure, Entertainments and Hotels sector on 17 January 2002.
>
> What does the table show?
>
> | Stock | Yield | P/E ratio |
> | --- | --- | --- |
> | Airtours | 3.7 | 27.8 |
> | Compass | 1.1 | 25.8 |
> | De Vere Group | 3.4 | 12.1 |
> | Holmes Place | 2.3 | 18.7 |
> | Manchester United | 1.4 | 24.8 |
> | Ryan Hotels | 11.1 | 4.4 |
> | Sunderland | 1.4 | 17.0 |
> | Wembley | 1.8 | 15.5 |

Clearly in deciding which companies to invest in an important consideration will be the dividend yields because these show returns on moneys invested.

6.3 IMPORTANT RATIOS FOR SHAREHOLDERS

Key Ideas 🔑

Additional share information

In addition to the traditional layout of the main stock page, newspapers typically provide additional information.

Major movers

Highlighted information is typically provided about the major risers and fallers in the FTSE 100 index, the techMARK shares, and other risers and fallers.

The techMARK is made up of shares in new companies which are representative of the 'new economy' – i.e. companies with a strong Information Technology and Internet base. This section of the market came to the fore in 2000 when people became very excited about the potential of these companies to form a 'new economy', replacing the 'old economy' made up of companies with traditional ways of carrying out business. The techMARK is the market for technology stocks.

On Thursday 17 January 2002 the following information was available:
(one example only from each category)

	price (p)	change (p)	change %
FTSE 100 risers			
Lattice	167	5	3.09
FTSE 100 fallers			
Logica	604	−40	−6.21
techMARK risers			
Vtech	57	8.5	17.53
techMARK fallers			
Xansa	302.5	−46.5	−13.32

Other useful information shown to readers is the FTSE 100 hour by hour:

17 January

Open	5166.0	
9.00	5140.3	−25.7
10.00	5145.6	5.3
11.00	5142.0	−3.6
12.00	5134.6	−7.4
13.00	5112.5	−22.1
14.00	5115.8	3.3
15.00	5130.4	14.6
16.00	5134.4	4.0
Close	5127.6	−6.8

Another useful set of information is a table showing the best and worst sectors on the previous day's trading:

Best +		Worst –	
Gas distribution	1.8	Information technology	−6.1
Tobacco	1.8	Software and computer services	−5.3
Personal & house products	1.6	Electronics and electrical	−5.2
Health	1.3	Steel and other metals	−4.4
Life assurance	0.8	Engineering	−2.5

Another useful indicator is the FTSE volumes indicator, showing the volumes of shares traded in a particular day. This shows which shares are being bought and sold in the greatest numbers.

6.4 FTSE AND OTHER INDEXES

Key Ideas O━

Share price indexes

Doctor Proctor outlines... HOW INDEXES ARE CALCULATED

To provide a measure of how values change over time, it is sometimes necessary to construct an **index**. Indexes are used to show average changes in share price over time.

The principle is to compare the value of items in the index against a **base value** determined for a **base period**.

For example, assume that an investor owns equal numbers of shares in three companies and wants to check on their average price change over time.

Starting with a base year of 2000:

Share	Price in 2000	Price in 2001	Increase in %
Superior Supermarket	100	150	50
Premier Football	60	75	25
Better Hotels	50	60	20

To work out the indexed increase we simply give each of the years a base figure of 100 and then measure the change in price relative to this base:

Doctor Proctor Calculates

	Base 2000	New figure 2001	
Superior Supermarket	100	150	(50% increase)
Premier Football	100	125	(25% increase)
Better Hotels	100	120	(20% increase)

To find out the average increase we simply need to add together the new figures for 2001 and divide by the number of shares, i.e.

$(150 + 125 + 120) = 395$

Number of shares $= 3$

Average increase $= \frac{395}{3} = 131.66$

The share price index for these shares has thus risen from 100 to 131.66 – an average increase of just over 30%.

6.4 FTSE AND OTHER INDEXES

Key Ideas

FTSE indexes

The **FTSE (Footsie) 100 index** gives hourly market movements for the most significant 100 companies on the London market. It is used as an indicator of the health of the economy. This index started with a base of 1,000.

FTSE 100 as at 15 January 2002

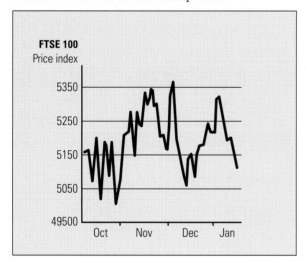

The **FTSE 250 index** is made up of the next range of companies, just below the size that would qualify them for the FTSE 100. The **FTSE 350** combines the 100 and the 250 index. There are separate indexes for smaller companies. The **FTSE techMark index** tracks the progress of technology related stocks.

The **FTSE all share index** covers all listed companies. Within the European Union, the most important indexes are the **Eurotop 100** and the **Eurotop 200**, which as the names suggest are made up of key shares in the European Union. **The Dow Jones Industrial Average** covers the New York Stock Exchange and the **Nikkei 225** covers the Tokyo market.

Movements in an index are usually referred to as points; for example, if the FTSE 100 falls from 5350 to 5250, it is said to have fallen 100 points.

Share price indices are regularly altering. Investors are generally happy when the index is moving upwards but will worry if the index starts to fall. Stock market indices go through a series of peaks and troughs which are representative of changes in the wider economy.

Share prices generally are likely to fall when there is a widespread loss of confidence in the world economy, such as that which occurred following the terrorist attack on the World Trade Center in New York on 11 September 2001. At such times, the number of people wishing to sell shares will exceed the number wanting to buy shares.

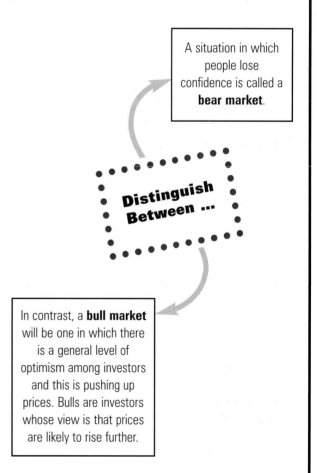

A situation in which people lose confidence is called a **bear market**.

Distinguish Between ...

In contrast, a **bull market** will be one in which there is a general level of optimism among investors and this is pushing up prices. Bulls are investors whose view is that prices are likely to rise further.

6.4 FTSE AND OTHER INDEXES

Doctor Proctor outlines... WHEN SHARE PRICES WILL RISE

When are share prices likely to rise?

- When company profits are announced and they prove to be higher than expected. Share prices often rise just before the announcement of profits in anticipation of high profits. Should these expectations prove to be unfounded, prices will probably fall.

- When they yield or are expected to yield good returns over time. Look for shares with a high P/E ratio.

- When a company is moving into a new area, or expanding in an existing area where there are clear opportunities – e.g. moving into new geographical locations or product areas.

- When the share price has been undervalued relative to the ability of the company to yield future profits.

- When the yield on alternative investments falls – e.g. if interest rates fall then equities (which pay dividends) may appear that much more attractive.

- When there is a general level of optimism in the economy that things will get better.

- When there is a high level of interest in a company and its shares, perhaps fuelled by media interest.

- When share prices in other world markets are increasing. For example, an increase in the Dow Jones and the Nikkei will make UK investors more confident.

- During periods of takeovers; one company taking over another will help to boost demand for shares, pushing up prices. In 'takeover booms' speculators will invest in shares when they think a takeover is possible.

6.5 COMPANY AND GOVERNMENT BONDS

Key Ideas

Bonds

A bond is basically a loan. The owner of the bond has given the issuer a sum of money. In return the issuer pays interest to the bondholder over a period of time and will eventually return the initial amount loaned, called the principal. The bondholder does not own a part of a company. As well as companies, the government also issues bonds to finance its expenditure needs.

Bonds are sometimes referred to as **fixed interest securities**. When the bond is issued the lender knows the fixed rate of interest that they will receive.

The following details are typically set out in bond certificates:

1   the time to maturity – i.e it will set out the date at which time the principal will be repaid to the lender;

2   the principal or par value – i.e. the amount that will be returned to the bondholder at maturity, e.g. £1,000;

3   the interest payment that will be paid on an annual basis to the bondholder.

Typical bonds are:

• Company bonds

• Local government bonds

• Central government bonds.

Gilt-edged stock is the term used to describe government stocks. They are regarded to be gilt edged because the owners of these bonds can be certain of repayment. New issues of gilt edged stock are made to replace maturing bonds.

When the government issues new bonds it does so at the prevailing market rate of interest, e.g. 5%. An investor would therefore hold a £100 bond with a market rate of interest of 5% (£5 a year), perhaps to be redeemed in 2009. If interest rates in the economy then rise to 10%, for example, the holder of the bond would be receiving less than the market rate of interest. The market price of the bond will therefore have to fall to £50 – a price at which the £5 interest paid each year would be 10%.

The price of fixed interest government stock therefore rises and falls in inverse proportion to prevailing interest rates.

Most stocks are offered in units of £100. Short stocks have a life of less than five years before the government redeems them, mediums last between five and fifteen years, and longs exceed fifteen years; some stocks are undated. 'High' and 'low' record the highest and lowest prices the stocks have reached during the year. The price of each stock is quoted in pounds. The plus or minus symbols (+/−) record the rise or fall in price from the close of trading on the previous day.

6.5 COMPANY AND GOVERNMENT BONDS

Gilt-edged stock (prices in early 2002)

High	Low	Stock	Price	Change	
PERPETUAL					
54.76	48.2	Con 2.5% Perp	50.14	0.34	Perpetuals are bonds on which there is no stated maturity date. Their price is therefore relatively low.
SHORTS					
103.4	100.09	Con 9.5% 02	100.1	0.01	Shorts will shortly be repaid and therefore their price will be very close to £100.
MEDIUMS					
107.61	103.81	Treasury 6.75% 04	105.11	0.03	Medium-term shares have longer to be repaid – in this case 2004. Because the rate of interest on these is higher than the market rate, in early 2002 they traded at over £100.
LONGS					
139.17	130.06	Treasury 9% 12	133.78	0.5	These have the greatest length before they are redeemed – in this case 2012. Since at the time of issue the market rate of interest was 9%, they now trade at £133.78.

The Financial Times publishes a government securities index. The nearer a bond gets to its redemption date, the nearer the price will be to its face value.

6.6 MANAGED FUND PRICES

Key Ideas 🔑

Unit trust prices

The financial press typically has a page showing developments in the fortunes of managed funds such as investment trusts and unit trusts, which were described earlier in Unit 2. The following notes relate specifically to unit trust reporting as representing managed funds in general.

The monthly magazine *Money Management* provides a comprehensive list showing the value of £1,000 invested over periods ranging from six months to seven or ten years, and various Internet websites also provide performance information.

Some unit trusts are designed to produce a regular income in the form of yields, while others only produce money when they are sold because their shares have risen in value considerably.

Each unit trust holds a portfolio of shares. Trust funds are legally owned by their managers but the benefit goes to the individual investors, who trust the managers to invest their money wisely.

Trust fund managers control a number of trusts, each one of which has its own name; some trusts specialise in particular groups of shares.

In the financial pages, 'sell' is the price obtained on the stock market when you sell a trust fund; 'buy' is the price you have to pay to obtain one; '+/–' is the rise or fall in the buying price of the fund each day. The yield is the income which owners receive from their trust funds; interest from each share in the fund is used to buy more shares and therefore increase the yield. Yield is expressed as the annual percentage return on each fund.

Example

The following figures show details of figures presented for Halifax Unit Trust Management Ltd in the Managed Funds section of a national newspaper:

Fund	Sell	Buy	+/–	Yield
Ethical Retail	79.02*		–0.48	1.38
European Retail	137.55*		+0.34	1.38
Far Eastern Retail	282.79*		+0.88	0.99

*This represents the middle value between the selling and buying price

Section 6.1: Reading the Financial Pages of a Newspaper

1 The profits of a Premier League Football club have risen steadily in each of the last three years. Explain the impact that this is likely to have on the share price over time. What other factors might have influenced share price?

2 Why might an investor prefer to hold equities rather than the loan stock of a company?

Section 6.2: Buying and Selling Equities

The following extract appeared on the share page of a national newspaper on the 17 January 2002:

Food and Drug Retailing Sector

High	Low	Stock	Price	Change	Yield	P/E
110	66	Budgens	102.0	1.0	2.6	19.7
220	178	**Morrison W**	198.0	0.0	0.9	22.8
419	286	**Safeway**	310.5	3.5	3.0	12.0
448	327	**Sainsbury**	385.0	9.5	3.7	21.0
271	229	Thorntons	101.0	0.0	6.7	16.9

1 Which share price has shown the greatest fluctuation over the twelve month period? Why might this be the case?

2 Which of these share prices would be represented in the FTSE 100 index?

3 Which share appears to have the greatest growth prospects?

4 Which share price has risen the most since the previous day? Why might this be the case?

5 List two other sectors that would appear on the share page of a national newspaper.

Section 6.3: Important ratios for shareholders

1 What is the formula for earnings per share? What does this ratio show?

2 What other method can be used for measuring returns to shareholders?

3 What is the price/earnings ratio? What does a high price/earnings ratio indicate?

Section 6.4: FTSE and Other Indexes

1 What is the FTSE 100 Index? How does this differ from the FTSE 250 index?

2 What are the names of the share indexes in the United States and Japan?

3 Explain two factors that might lead to a fall in the FTSE all share index.

Section 6.5: Company and Government Bonds

1 What are gilt-edged stock? Why are the prices of some gilt-edged stock higher than others?

2 What is the relationship between the market rate of interest and the price of bonds?

Section 6.6: Managed Fund Prices

1 What is a unit trust? How do unit trusts help investors to spread risks?

2 What is the difference between income and growth?

┌──────────────────────────┐
: UNIT 7 :
:   :
: FINANCIAL :
: INFORMATION IN THE :
: MEDIA – COMMODITY :
: AND FINANCIAL :
: TRADING :
└──────────────────────────┘

Topics covered in this unit

7.1 Commodity Trading
Describes the main types of hard and soft commodities that are traded through organised exchanges in the City of London. Explains the role of spot and futures markets and how prices are presented in the media.

7.2 LIFFE Options and Financial Futures
Describes the work of the London International Financial Futures Exchange and explains the difference between futures and options.

7.3 Interest Rates
Explains the nature of interest rates and the different types of interest rates that exist and how these are presented in the media.

7.4 Exchange Rates
Describes the importance of exchange rates in international trade, and the way in which different types of spot, forward and tourist rates are presented in the media.

Questions

This unit gives you an overview of the markets for commodities and financial futures, which are traded through organised markets. It shows how financial information about prices is presented in the financial press and other media.

7.1 COMMODITY TRADING

Key Ideas ⊶

Markets in the City of London

In addition to the Stock Exchange, there are several other markets in the City of London and elsewhere that are the centres for trading in a range of commodities such as metals and agricultural produce, as well as in financial futures and options.

The London exchanges originally concentrated on metals and soft commodities but have developed, over the years, to deal with a much wider range of commodities. However, in the last thirty years there has been rapid growth in financial futures and options, trading globally, covering mainly interest rate, bond and equity related products.

Taking risks

There is an element of risk in any activity when the outcome cannot be predicted with certainty, or when the outcome is known but its full consequences are not. Individuals have widely different attitudes towards taking risks. It is possible to identify three different positions:

1   The **risk lover** – someone who enjoys a gamble, even when mathematical analysis shows that the odds are unfavourable.

2   The **risk-neutral person** – will only speculate if the odds on gain are favourable. The person will not be concerned with the range of possible outcomes, only with the odds being in their favour.

3   The **risk-averse person** – will not leave anything to chance and only speculates if the odds are strongly favourable.

In business, organisations also take risks. Some are prepared to take large risks which can make or break the organisation but more typically, organisations aim to manage their risks.

Doctor Proctor outlines... COMMODITIES

Commodities lie at the heart of modern industrial society and include a wide range of primary products ranging from foodstuffs, such as rice, grain and coffee, to industrial raw materials, such as oil and iron ore. At exchanges based in London, dealers buy and sell contracts for large quantities of raw materials. Some of the dealers are acting for firms purchasing commodities for their factories, others for speculators hoping to make a quick profit by selling their contract on to another dealer.

The prices of commodities change over time, due to changing supply and demand conditions in the marketplace. For example, more oil than normal may be consumed during a particularly cold winter and so demand increases; frosts may destroy olive trees in southern Italy; potato blight may wipe out a crop in the east of England, political upheavals in the Middle East may prevent the free flow of oil.

Examples

The **London Commodity Exchange** is part of the Futures and Options Exchange (FOX), situated in the east of the City of London; it trades in contracts for cocoa, coffee and sugar.

The **International Petroleum Exchange (IPE)** buys and sells oil and gas. **Brent** is the main oilfield in the North Sea and therefore of vital importance to the British economy; the price quoted is in dollars for a barrel of crude oil.

The **Baltic Exchange** is a market for shipping and agricultural products. For example, a company wishing to transport grain to this country can charter a vessel on the Baltic Exchange.

The **London Metal Exchange** buys and sells all metals except iron, steel and gold.

7.1 COMMODITY TRADING

In the commodities markets, the main buyers will be large companies involved in a particular industry – e.g. chocolate manufacturers buying cocoa, oil refiners buying crude oil, etc.

Let us take the example of oil trading to show how buying and selling can take place.

Distinguish Between ...

Term deals

Spot deals

Doctor Proctor outlines... TRADING IN THE OIL MARKET

In the oil market trading deals can be either 'spot' or 'term'.

The main advantage of term dealing is to secure supply and reduce the risk the company has when the market is tight.

Term deals are usually agreed for a regular supply of an agreed quantity of a specified product (e.g. crude oil), over an extended period of time. The price of a term contract is usually a relationship to an agreed yardstick, such as prices in a given market journal, or a futures market price, rather than the market price prevailing at the time of the deal. The price is thus a 'floating price'.

The alternative to dealing on a term basis is to deal on a **spot** basis. Here, the trader buys or sells individual, specific cargoes as and when required. Spot deals are usually agreed on a floating price based on the market at a particular moment in time. Rotterdam's (the centre of the world oil market) daily spot prices are taken as reference in all spot transactions carried out on that day.

7.1 COMMODITY TRADING

Key Ideas 🔑

Trading in the futures market

Futures markets

When reading the Stock Exchange pages of a newspaper you will see that a key distinction is made between the spot and the futures price.

A **Future** is a contract to buy or sell a standard quantity of a specific commodity or financial instrument on a fixed date in the future at a price agreed today.

Futures trading can be applied to most things, which stand to rise or fall in value over a period of time.

The following table shows future prices for agricultural commodities at 5pm on 16 January 2002.

For example, the main commodity products traded on the futures markets in London include:

- cocoa
- coffee
- potatoes
- sugar (white)
- grain
- freight futures (referred to as BIFFEX)
- metals
- gas and oil

In addition to commodities, futures trading today takes place for a wide range of securities and currencies. Organisations with long-term needs for commodities can reduce price uncertainties by taking out a futures contract. This guarantees supply or purchase of the commodity at an agreed future date and at a price which reflects current thinking on the way prices will move. For example, organisations which require large quantities of a certain commodity (Burger King needs vast quantities of potato chips, Nestlé requires coffee beans, etc.) will seek to take advantage of the futures market by fixing their future price for buying potatoes, coffee beans and aluminium, etc. In a similar way, organisations exposed to interest rate movements or price changes on the Stock Exchange will benefit from using the futures market.

Cocoa		Coffee		Barley		Potatoes		Soya Beans	
Date	*£/tonne*	*Date*	*$/tonne*	*Date*	*£/tonne*	*Date*	*£/tonne*	*Date*	*$/tonne*
Mar 02	1002.00	Mar 02	383.00	Jan 02	63.70	Mar 02	125.00	Mar 02	445.00
May 02	1009.00	May 02	395.00	Mar 02	65.00	Apr 02	140.00	May 02	450.00
Jul 02	1020.00	Jul 02	409.00	May 02	67.20	May 02	150.00	Jul 02	454.25

White Sugar		Wheat		Corn		Large Potatoes	
Date	*$/tonne*	*Date*	*£/tonne*	*Date*	*Cents/bshl*	*Date*	*$/25kg*
Mar 02	250.50	Jan 02	78.30	Mar 02	212.50	Apr 02	22.40
May 02	233.30	Mar 02	80.0	May 02	219.50	Jun 02	26.30
Aug 02	212.20	May 02	81.50	Jul 02	226.25		

7.1 COMMODITY TRADING

Typically, the further we move into the future the higher the prices for futures contracts because of the bigger risk/greater uncertainty. However, this does not have to be the case with agricultural commodities because of the timing of harvests, e.g. in the case of sugar.

The energy market shows a similar picture:

Energy at 5pm on 16 January 2002

Brent Crude ($/barrel)

IPE	Last	Change
March	18.68	−0.29
April	18.92	−0.23
May	19.05	−0.17

These figures show that the further into the future we go, the higher the price for futures oil becomes because of increasing uncertainty. The price of Brent Crude on the IPE was less than $20 at the time.

Over time the price of commodities will alter and it is important to understand these longer term price movements.

The Goldman Sachs commodity price index tracks changes in commodity prices against a base date (when average price is set at 100). The following table for 17 January 2002 indicates a general fall in commodity prices over time (as would be expected following 11 September).

Goldman Sachs commodity indices (at 5pm on 17 January)

	Base date	Last	Change	% Change	31Dec	% Change year to date
Index	1970 = 100	167.48	−0.59	−0.35	215.26	−22.20
Agricultural	1970 = 100	167.70	−0.01	−0.01	231.23	−29.64
Energy	1983 = 100	68.62	−0.34	−0.49	85.86	−20.08
Ind Metals	1977 = 100	138.83	0.00	0.00	168.79	−17.75
Livestock	1970 = 100	190.77	−0.35	−0.18	191.03	−0.14
Prec Metals	1973 = 100	384.04	2.45	0.64	463.54	−17.15

In addition to futures, dealers also buy and sell under another type of contract known as an **Option**.

An option is where the dealer takes out an option on a futures contract, and will only buy or sell if it is profitable; the dealer loses the initial purchase price of the option if he or she does not finalise the contract, but can make a large profit if the commodity price rises sharply.

7.1 COMMODITY TRADING

Hedging

Most large organisations buying particular commodities know that they will need a regular supply of the products over a long period of time. These organisations may need to replenish supplies on a regular basis with cover for three, six or nine months time, during which time the price of that commodity may have substantially increased due to, for example, a harvest failure or a natural disaster in a key supplier country. In order to take some of the risk out of future purchases, it is possible to hedge. Hedging involves matching the sale or purchase of commodities with an opposite transaction (i.e. the purchase or sale of a similar quantity of the same product) on the futures market.

Speculators

Speculators are a key feature of many modern markets. Speculators try to make a profit by predicting future changes in prices. Speculators play a key role in commodity trading. A speculator is not concerned with the physical delivery of anything – they would not want 10,000 tonnes of potatoes! Instead, the speculator is more concerned about buying/selling on the contracts that they make in international exchange at a considerable gain. A speculator fits into the category of the 'risk lover'. They seek to make a quick profit through successful futures transactions.

Example

Here is an example of hedging:

A company contracts to sell potatoes in six months time at the current **spot** price, being the price currently obtainable. However, the company is concerned that when the time comes to honour the contract, the price of potatoes will have risen. As a result, the company will lose money, either because it could have sold its potatoes at the higher price or because it will itself have to buy potatoes at the higher price to honour its contract. To protect itself against that possible loss, the company contracts to buy a similar amount of potatoes at the price that the market thinks will be obtainable in six months' time (in other words, it buys a six months' 'future' in potatoes). So, whether the price of potatoes rises or falls, the company will not lose money (nor, of course, will it make money if the price rises – other than the profit built into the original contract).

7.2 LIFFE OPTIONS AND FINANCIAL FUTURES

Key Ideas 🔑

LIFFE

The London International Financial Futures and Options Exchange or LIFFE is one of the largest in the world. Like dealers in commodity markets, dealers in the London Financial Futures Exchange buy and sell contracts in financial commodities, such as foreign currencies or shares.

LIFFE dealers trade futures contracts and options at a price agreed now in the hope of making a profit in the future. The financial futures and options market is the most intense and competitive of them all, for it is possible to make, or lose, millions of pounds speculating on the future performance of international finance.

Doctor Proctor outlines... HOW LIFFE OPTIONS WORK

An option is where the dealer takes out an option on a futures contract, speculating that the price of the financial commodity will rise so that he makes a profit on the deal; if the price falls, the dealer only loses the initial contract payment. Options can be taken out for a specific number of shares of major companies, listed with their current share prices in brackets underneath their name. The options for each company are quoted either side of its share price, presuming that the price will rise or fall to that level in the future.

Calls are the options to buy at 3 three month intervals in the future, and are usually bought in the expectation of a rising price.

Puts are the options to sell at 3 three month intervals in the future, and are usually bought in the expectation of a falling price.

The prices listed in pence in the calls and puts columns are the prices paid when the dealer takes out an option to buy or sell a futures contract; if the dealer does not take up the option he loses this amount.

The following is taken from the LIFFE Equity Options page of a national newspaper for 27 January 2002, showing calls and puts for Abbey National and Allied Domecq shares:

Option	Calls			Puts		
	Apr	*Jul*	*Oct*	*Apr*	*Jul*	*Oct*
Abbey National 1050	58.5	82.0	103.5	59.0	83.0	109.0
(*1064) 1100	35.0	60.5	83.0	90.5	112.0	139.0
Allied Domecq 390	23.0	32.5	39.5	17.5	27.0	32.0
(*392) 420	10.5	20.0	27.0	35.5	45.0	49.5

*indicates underlying security price. Premiums shown are based on settlement price

7.2 LIFFE OPTIONS AND FINANCIAL FUTURES

With the current share price of Abbey National at 1064, speculators can buy options in the share price falling to 1050 or rising to 1100. The further into the future the speculation falls, the greater the chance of profits or losses.

As well as being able to speculate against future prices of individual shares, speculators can also take out options on the overall performance of the Stock Exchange. The current index of prices on the exchange is listed, along with a range, either side of which it can be taken up as an option.

Futures can be taken out on the performance of leading companies on the Stock Exchange, on the exchange rate of the pound and other currencies, and on government bonds or loans.

7.3 INTEREST RATES

Key Ideas

Interest rate

Money is a commodity just like potatoes or oil. It has a price at which it can be bought or borrowed, and a price at which it can be exchanged.

Banks have money to lend, and charge borrowers an interest rate, which varies according to the size and length of the loan.

Doctor Proctor outlines... INTEREST RATES

Interest is the amount charged by a lender to a borrower for a sum of money.

The Bank of England's **Monetary Policy Committee** meets each month to set the interest rate set by the Bank. Other financial institutions (e.g. high street banks) set their interest rates in line with the Bank of England's base rate. They will charge a higher rate of interest and the amount they charge depends on the risk they are taking and the need to compete with rivals. The more risky a bank's customer is, the higher the rate of interest they will have to pay to borrow money.

Treasury Bills are short-term bills issued by the government to finance their short-term borrowing requirements, e.g. for 91 days.

Discount market loans, Treasury bills, prime bank bills, Sterling money rates and Interbank are all different systems by which banks lend money to each other; the loans can be bought and sold and the interest rate varies according to the length of the loan.

A **CD** is a certificate of deposit issued by one bank to another one that deposits money in it, in order to earn a good rate of interest; CDs can be bought and sold.

European money deposits are the interest rates given by British banks for deposits of foreign currencies.

Local authority deposits are loans made to local councils to enable them to finance their spending on such things as roads and houses.

The price of **gold bullion** and other **precious metals** such as platinum, silver and palladium is important because when people are uncertain about the value of money, they like to invest their money in gold. **Krugerrands** are gold coins from South Africa made of one troy ounce of pure gold.

7.3 INTEREST RATES

The following tables set out money rates on 17 January 2002:

Money rates %

Base rates:	Clearing banks 4	Finance houses 5
Discount market loans:	Overnight high 3.5	
Treasury bills (discount rate)	Buy: 2 month 3.76,	3 month 3.76
	Sell: 2 month 3.66,	3 month 3.66

	1 mth	*2 mths*	*3 mths*	*6 mths*	*12 mths*
Interbank rates	3.83–3.78	3.89–3.84	3.92–3.87	3.95–3.90	4.14–4.09
Clearer CDs	3.81–3.78	3.87–3.84	3.89–3.86	3.92–3.89	4.12–4.09
Depo CDs	3.80–3.77	3.86–3.83	3.88–3.85	3.91–3.88	4.11–4.09

Local authority deposits	3.75	n/a	3.75	3.75	4
Eurodollar deposits	2.5–2.2	n/a	2.6–2.3	2.7–2.4	2.8–2.5
Eurodollar CDs	2.04	n/a	2.05	2.11	2.56

European money deposits %

Currency	1 mth	3 mths	6 mths	12 mths	Call
Dollar	2.10–1.97	2.15–2.02	2.22–2.09	2.64–2.51	2–2

Gold/precious metals

Bullion: Open $273.25–273.75   Close $272.50–273.00

Krugerrand: $272.00–$275.00

Platinum: $437.00   Silver: $4.05   Palladium: $333.00

7.4 EXCHANGE RATES

Key Ideas 🔑

Spot and forward rates

Businesses need to protect theselves against the effect of swings in the values of currencies by hedging their currency risks. There is a forward market in currencies as well as a **spot** market.

If a British company currently holds sterling but knows that it will have to pay for imports from Germany in Euros in three months time, and is worried that the value of the Euro will rise, it can buy Euros today for delivery in three months' time. In this way it is locking in to a known exchange rate.

Foreign exchange is dealt in by the major banks and by specialist foreign exchange brokers, working on the **Forex markets** that operate from screen cluttered trading floors.

The financial media quote a sterling (pound) exchange rate against a number of major world currencies.

The **spot rate** is the rate at which the pound is traded for exchange with another currency within two days; **range** is the high and low during the day, while **close** indicates the rate at close of trading.

The **forward rate** is the rate at which the pound is traded for exchange with another currency one and three months in the future; **premium** indicates the amount added to the rate, **discount** the amount taken away.

Because the Euro and the US dollar are such important currencies in world finance today, the Euro and dollar rates are quoted against a range of international currencies.

The following table shows sterling rates against various currencies on 16 January 2002:

Foreign Exchange Rates					
Country	**Sterling spot**	**1 month**	**Dollar spot**	**1 month**	**Euro**
UK	1.000		0.6957	0.6971	0.6147
Australia	2.7869	2.7796	1.9389	1.9378	1.7131
Canada	2.2939	2.2899	1.5959	1.5964	1.4101
Denmark	12.086	12.082	8.4088	8.4228	7.4296
Euro	1.6268	1.6258	1.1318	1.1334	1.0000

Tourist rates

Another useful source of information for travellers is the current tourist exchange rate. The rate of exchange is set out in terms of how many units of currency one British pound will buy.

Exemplar tourist rates, on 26 January 2002			
Australia ($)	2.6971	Japan (yen)	185.56
Euro (€)	1.5795	USA ($)	1.4065
India (rupees)	62.51		

Bank buys is the rate at which the bank buys foreign currency from you when you return home from abroad.

Bank sells is the rate at which the bank sells you foreign currency when you go abroad.

Banks make a profit on the difference between the amount at which they buy and sell currency.

Section 7.1: Commodity Trading

The table below shows crude oil prices on the IPE in the week ending 26/27 January 2002.

Crude oil IPE ($/barrel)

	Settlement price	Day's change	High	Low
March	19.37	+0.24	19.60	18.77
April	19.50	+0.21	19.65	19.00
May	19.62	+0.27	19.64	19.10
June	20.46	+0.23	19.60	19.10

1 What has happened to oil futures since the previous day?

2 How might a report that refineries were going to cut back production have influenced this change?

3 How might continued mild weather in the US and Europe have affected oil futures?

4 In late January 2002 the key world rubber producers Indonesia and Thailand, which produce over half of the world's rubber, announced that they would be cutting back production. What do you think the impact will be on rubber futures?

Section 7.2: LIFFE Options and Financial Futures

1 What is the difference between a futures and an option contract?

2 Why are speculators likely to buy option contracts?

Section 7.3: Interest Rates

1 What is the body responsible for setting interest rates in this country?

2 How do high street banks decide on the level of interest that they charge customers?

3 What are a) Certificates of Deposit, b) Treasury Bills, c) Krugerrands?

Section 7.4: Exchange Rates

1 Why might an importer want to use the Forex market?

2 What is the difference between 'bank buys' and 'bank sells' in the tourist rates column of a national newspaper?

Doctor Proctor's Guide to Researching Financial Information

This book will have given you useful guidelines on how to read company reports and other sources of financial information presented in the media.

Equipped with this understanding, you will want to carry out some independent research. There are so many different sources that you can turn to that I have decided to narrow this down to a list of indicative sources; these will provide you with more than enough information.

1 Company reports

Company reports can be obtained direct from the company secretary or public relations department of a public limited company. Alternatively, simply surf the net, entering the name of the company you are seeking information about, e.g. Shell UK, Tesco, etc. Each company's website will generally give financial highlights, the Chair and/or Chief Executive's Report and the Directors' Report, including the balance sheet, and profit and loss account.

World Investor Link

The Annual Reports Service enables you to research one company, ten companies or entire industry sectors completely free. Reports are usually sent out within forty-eight hours. Companies are listed under industry sectors and reports can be ordered by filling in an application form, ticking off relevant reports.

The address is: World Investor Link, Unit 1 HQ3, Hook Rise South, South Surbiton, Surrey, KT6 7LD.

You can order reports online through Hemmington Scott at www.hemscott.net, which simply involves ticking boxes online.

Company reports can also be ordered through World Investor Link, using the Financial Times site **FT.com**. Ordering online is through http://ft.ar.wilink.com or www.annualreports.ft.com/

In addition, company reports can be viewed on-line at www.carol.co.uk/

2 Information for investors

There are many magazine and journal sources of information for investors. Today, these are accompanied by an appropriate website.

A useful journal for those wanting to research the latest developments in corporate governance is *Corporate Governance* (which would be available from a specialist University library).

Another specialist publication on company reporting is: *Company Reporting* (available at www.companyreporting.com).

There are lots of magazines available for professional investors that generally examine issues related to equities and other forms of investment, looking at economic forecasts and changes in the market.

Examples are:

Investors Chronicle (www.investorschronicle.co.uk)

Bloomberg Money (www.bloomberg.com/uk)

In addition to its magazine sold through newsagents like WH Smith, the core product of Bloomberg is the **Bloomberg Professional**, a computer application that resides on the desktop to provide the definitive source of real-time pricing, news, data, historical information and analysis on the global financial markets. The service is available 24 hours a day to more than 250,000 professionals in over one hundred countries. Bloomberg has a range of media products including:

- 24 hour TV in a number of languages
- magazines
- radio
- localised websites.

Other business news services for investors are provided by news agencies such as:

> www.bbc.co.uk/
> www.economist.com/
> www.euromoney.com/
> www.newsunlimited.co.uk/
> www.independent.co.uk/
> www.reuters.com/
> www.sunday-times.co.uk/
> www.telegraph.co.uk/
> www.the-times.co.uk/

www.InvestorsGuide.com/ is the website of *Investors Guide Daily*, which provides a free investing and financial newsletter, e-mailed to you each day.

A specialist journal for the professional investor is *Professional Investor*, which is the official journal of the UK society of Investment Professionals. Its website is:

> www.uksip.org/

The Motley Fool provides a lot of up-to-date information about different forms of investment, and gives suggestions to investors in a series of books and on its website:

> www.fool.com/

An organisation specifically set up to encourage share buying in this country is ProShare and its website provides a wealth of information at:

> www.proshare.org.uk

3 Exchanges and markets

There are several useful websites for finding out information about the various markets for shares, commodities, foreign exchange, money, financial futures, etc.

> www.crestco.co.uk/
> The CREST settlement system

> www.forexia.com/
> Foreign exchange (Thomas Cook)

> www.ftse.com/
> FTSE International (indices)

> www.ipe.uk.com/
> International Petroleum Exchange (IPE)

> www.liffe.com/
> LIFFE

> www.lloydsoflondon.co.uk/
> Lloyds of London

> www.lme.co.uk/
> London Metal Exchange

> www.londonstockexchange.com/
> London Stock Exchange

> www.nasdaq.com/
> NASDAQ

> www.ofex.co.uk/
> OFEX

> www.sets.co.uk/
> SETS (London trading system)

> www.simple.com/
> Mutuals

4 Government websites

The government provides a range of statistics and information relating to financial issues, the control of companies and corporate governance.

Key sites are:

> www.asb.org.uk/
> Accounting Standards Board

> www.bankofengland.co.uk/
> Bank of England

> www.coi.gov.uk/
> Central Office of Information

> www.cityoflondon.gov.uk/
> City of London

> www.companieshouse.gov.uk/
> Companies House

> www.frc.org.uk/
> Financial Reporting Council

> www.frrp.org.uk/
> Financial Reporting Review Panel

> www.inlandrevenue.gov.uk/
> Inland Revenue

> www.hm-treasury.gov.uk/
> Treasury

> www.statistics.gov.uk/
> UK Official Statistics

Answers

Unit 2: The Importance of the Company

What is a company?

- A public company (plc) sells its shares on the Stock Exchange. Shares can be bought freely. A private company (Ltd) does not sell shares through the Stock Exchange, shares can be traded only with the permission of the Board of Directors.
- Ltd refers to a private company; Plc to a public company.
- A sole trader has one owner who is personally responsible for the debts of the business. A partnership can have two or more partners who share responsibility for running the business, share profits, and are jointly accountable for debts.
- Limited liability protects the owners of a business so that they are liable for are debts up to the value of their shareholding in a business. Sole traders and partners (with the exception of limited partnerships) have unlimited liability, meaning that they must meet the full debts of their business.

Controlling the activities of companies

Articles	Memorandum of Association
Details of how long directors keep their posts	Company objectives
The voting rights of shareholders	Amounts of different types of shares
Where or how the chair will be appointed	Registered office of the company
Details of the AGM.	

The role of directors

1. False (not always)
2. False (collective responsibility)
3. True
4. True
5. True
6. True

The role of the Stock Exchange

1. The Stock Exchange Council
2. In the 'Yellow Book', *Admissions of Securities to Listing*
3. Merchant banks
4. Because the merchant bank recommends them and places them with a share-buying institution prior to launch.
5. The official list includes shares with a full listing on the Stock Exchange. The AIM (Alternative Investment Market) deals with newer shares, often in smaller companies that have not yet graduated to a full listing.

Unit trusts

When investors buy units in a unit trust they are, in effect, investing in a range of companies, because the trust uses the fund to buy shares in a selection of companies. Yield is the income that an investor receives from their trust fund, whereas growth is the increase in value of the trust over time.

Investment trusts

An individual can buy shares in an investment trust by writing directly to the investment trust and filling in an application form or by going through a broker. They can then either put a lump sum into the investment fund or pay in regular instalments. They gain because the investment trust spreads the risk by investing in a range of companies and then paying out a dividend. The investor also gains through the growth in value of the investment trust over time.

Types of shares

1. True – it is easier to offer a rights issue or new shares because the company's name is known.
2. False – preferential debtors such as owners of preference shares are paid first before ordinary shareholders.
3. False – equity is the capital provided by ordinary shareholders.
4. False – the authorised capital is what the company is allowed to raise; the issued capital is the part of this that has been raised at a particular moment in time.
5. True – directors are accountable to shareholders.

Sources of third party finance

1. Debentures are loans to companies which yield a fixed rate of interest. They are fixed interest securities which must be paid before ordinary shareholders can be paid.
2. Convertible loan stock are debentures that can be converted into shares at some future date.

Unit 3: Reading Company Reports

The main components of company reports

1. Stock Exchange rules, legal requirements, accounting standards, codes of best practice for corporate governance.

2   Directors' report, auditors' report, profit and loss account, balance sheet, cash flow statement, statement of total gains and losses, notes.

Financial highlights

The shareholders will be optimistic because turnover has improved steadily from just over £70m to over £185m. Profit before tax has risen from £15.6m to £40m. Perhaps most importantly the company has been able to pay increasingly higher dividends, rising from 3.35 pence in 1997 to 8.4 pence in 2001.

The Chairperson and Chief Executive's Report

1   These are not legal requirements although they typically appear in a company report. It is a legal requirement for directors to report to shareholders.
2   A pessimistic statement will lead to a loss of confidence so that share price may fall. An over-optimistic evaluation will push the share price up above the real value of the company.
3   The full range of stakeholders – e.g. tax officials, competitors, customers, suppliers, employees, etc.

Directors' Report and Corporate Governance Report

1   Typically this statement would appear in the corporate governance section of the report.
2   It is compulsory to produce a directors' report.
3   Accountability involves being held up to scrutiny and giving a full account of corporate governance and the running of the company. A statement on corporate governance gives a clear idea of how the company is organised and controlled.

Auditing company reports

Four key elements:

1   Title setting out who is being addressed in the report, i.e. shareholders.
2   Introductory paragraph setting out the financial statements that have been audited.
3   Sections setting out responsibilities between directors and auditors. The basis of the auditor's opinion. Auditor's opinion.
4   Auditor's signature and date.

The main types of financial statements

1   Profit and loss account.
2   Balance sheet.
3   Cash flow statement.

Unit 4: Financial Statements and Accounts

The profit and loss account

1   Profit and Loss Account for Superior Leisure at 31 December 2003

	£m
Turnover	350
Cost of sales	200
Gross profit	**150**
Administrative expenses	50
Operating profit	**100**
Interest payable	(10)
Profit before taxation	**90**
Taxation	(15)
Profit for the financial year (after tax)	**75**
Dividends	25
Profit retained	**50**

2   a) Turnover is the value of sales made.
    b) Cost of sales is the direct cost of making these sales.
    c) The expenses are the indirect costs of running the business, e.g. the administrative expenses such as marketing and postal costs.

The balance sheet

1   Assets are what the business owns or is owed, whereas liabilities are what the business owes.
2   Assets = Capital + Liabilities
3   Buildings and machinery are examples of tangible fixed assets.
4   Research and development, and the brand are examples of intangible fixed assets.
5   Least liquid is stock, next liquid are debtors, most liquid is cash.
6   Working capital = current assets – current liabilities. It shows how solvent the business is.
7   Total net assets of a business are equal to capital and reserves.

The cash flow statement

1   Typically, the main type of cash inflow comes from normal operating activities.
2   Other sources of cash inflow come from the disposal of assets, dividends received, interest received and trade loans.
3   Cash outflows would include interest paid, dividends paid, corporation tax and money spent on acquisitions.

Notes to the accounts

1 Historical cost is when assets and liabilities are valued at the cost prevailing when they were incurred.
2 Segmental analysis breaks down figures into relevant business segments, e.g. departments within a business, geographical areas, etc.
3 Other details that might appear in the notes could include profit on the sale of fixed assets, a breakdown showing the ingredients of staff costs, a statement showing tax paid, etc.

Reporting business changes

1 Exceptional costs may be one-off restructuring costs for a business, or costs involved in arranging a takeover of another business.
2 Exceptional items are items that do not usually occur and thus give a distorted picture of trends in the business. They are abnormalities which may make it look as if a business is doing better or less well than usual – therefore they need to be set aside when looking at long-term trends.

The auditor's opinion

1 The auditor's role is to verify that the accounts provide a true and fair picture of the business operations and financial standing in a particular time period. They independently verify the report. The auditor provides independent protection for shareholders and others.
2 Accounting standards need to be consistent in order to make comparisons from one year to the next and across companies.

Unit 5: Ratio Analysis

Introduction to ratio analysis

1 A financial ratio is a comparison of two items from the financial statements of a business.
2 By comparing financial ratios with benchmarks it is possible to compare company performance against the best in the field or the best parts of the company, in order to set high standards/targets.
3 A benchmark might be the best figures in the industry, or those achieved by the best department in a company.

Profitability ratios

$$\text{Profit margin} = \frac{\text{Operating profit}}{\text{Turnover}}$$

This has increased from about 3% in 1998 to about 5% in 2002. This could be because cost of sales as a percentage of turnover has fallen because of increased efficiencies, or because expenses have fallen as a percentage of turnover. More detailed research therefore

would need to be carried out to examine cost of sales, and expenses. Also it might be necessary to examine the different sections of operating activity, e.g. different building activities carried out by the firm to see which are the most profitable.

Liquidity ratios

	2000
Current assets	
Stocks	97
Debtors	600
Investments	826
Cash at bank/in hand	125
	1648
Creditors: amounts falling due within one year	(1604)
Net current assets	44

1 The figure for creditors is shown in brackets because this represents liabilities owed by the firm to creditors.
2 Working capital enables Bass to carry out its everyday operations such as paying wages, buying new stock, etc.
3 Current ratio is: 1648 : 1604
4 Acid test ratio is: 1551 : 1604

Return on capital ratios

1 The cost of capital is the financial return that investors expect on the capital they invest.
2 Return on equity is the return that shareholders actually receive – it should be at least equal to the cost of capital or shareholders might seek to transfer their investment elsewhere.
3 Return on equity is the return on shareholders' capital. Return on capital employed goes beyond this to include in capital all forms of third party capital. ROCE is thus the return on all capital employed in the business.

Gearing ratios

1 Shareholders in the Green company are taking the biggest risk because 75 per cent of the capital of the company is in fixed interest securities. This means that the shareholders are behind a long line of people who are due to be paid before them when it comes to sharing out the profits.
2 If the Green company continues to sell more preference shares and other forms of loan capital then it will have a lot of interest to pay back each year. When the profits are poor it may not be able to pay the interest payments.
3 Gearing ratio for Green is 3:1, and for Yellow 1:3.

Efficiency ratios

1   Debtor days are calculated by:

$$\text{Debtor days} = \frac{\text{Debtors}}{\text{Credit sales}} \times 365 \text{ days}$$

Creditor days are calculated by:

$$\text{Creditor days} = \frac{\text{Trade creditors}}{\text{Cost of Sales}} \times 365$$

Stock turnover is calculated by:

$$\text{Stock turnover} = \frac{\text{Cost of sales}}{\text{Stock}}$$

Utilisation of capital employed is calculated by:

$$\text{Utilisation of capital employed} = \frac{\text{Sales}}{\text{Capital employed}}$$

2   There is some cause for concern because according to the figures:

- Debtors on average are taking longer to pay up – 65 days in 2002 compared with 50 days in 2001.
- Stock is turning over more slowly – ten times in 2002 compared with fifteen times in 2001.
- Utilisation of capital employed has fallen from 1.5 to 1.2, suggesting that the capital of the firm is not being used as effectively to generate sales as before. Is the image of the firm and its products becoming dated?

Limitations of ratio analysis

Falling ratios such as profitability may be because the firm is investing more now in order to secure longer-term profits. It is not simply important to look at short-term indicators. Also, there may be key information missing from published accounts which masks what is really going on – distorting ratio analysis.

Unit 6: Financial Information in the Media – Company Shares and Bonds

Reading the financial pages of a newspaper

1   The share price is likely to rise because investors looking for good returns will seek to buy these shares, as will investors interested in growth. This will lead to a high P/E ratio, which will encourage further buying and price increases.

2   Equities carry a greater risk but they also stand to gain the greatest share of the profits in good years. Equity holders will also have better voting rights and other preferential advantages compared with loan stock holders.

Buying and selling equities

1   Safeway has fluctuated by 133 points and Sainsbury has fluctuated by 121 points. This may be because trading figures have fluctuated over the period concerned, or the businesses may have been involved in takeover discussions. Returns on the share may also have improved or deteriorated.

2   Morrison W, Safeway and Sainsbury, as highlighted by the bold type.

3   Morrison W and Sainsbury have the highest P/E ratios.

4   Sainsbury has risen by 9.5, which is a reflection of the good trading results at the time and gains made against the market leader Tesco.

5   Aerospace and Defence, Automobiles, Banks, Beverages, Chemicals, etc.

Important ratios for shareholders

1

$$\text{Earnings per share (EPS)} = \frac{\text{Net profit (after tax and preference dividend)}}{\text{Average number of ordinary shares in issue}}$$

This shows how much profit is made on each individual share in the company, which is of interest to shareholders.

2   Dividend yield,

i.e. $\dfrac{\text{Dividend per share}}{\text{Share price}} \times 100$

3   The P/E ratio shows how many years it will take for current earnings to pay for a share in the company. It is measured by price/earnings. It is a good indicator of how quickly a company is growing.

FTSE and other indexes

1   The FTSE 100 index is an index with a base of 1000, stating the top 100 companies listed on the Stock Exchange. The FTSE 250 is made up of the next 250 companies.

2   Dow Jones and Nikkei.

3   A general level of pessimism about the economy or a sudden negative shock would lead to a fall in the all share index.

Company and government bonds

1   Gilt-edged stock are government bonds. They are gilt edged because they are sure of repayment, being backed by the government. The price of the stock on the open market depends on their nearness to repayment. The nearer to repayment they get, the closer they are to their face value. In addition, their price depends on the interest they pay, which is determined by the prevailing market rate of interest when they were issued.

2   The higher the market rate of interest when gilts are issued, the lower their price is likely to be in trade, although other factors like closeness to redemption are important.

Managed fund prices

1 A unit trust is a trust fund managed by professional investors and the trust holds a portfolio of shares. These trusts help the investor to spread risks by buying shares in a number of sectors and in a number of individual companies.

2 Income is the annual return on shares in the form of a dividend (or interest), whereas growth is concerned with the increase in the value of shares or in units.

Unit 7: Financial Information in the Media – Commodity and Financial Trading

Commodity trading

1 The price has risen, although it is below the high for the year.

2 A cutback in oil production reduces supply, forcing an increase in price.

3 The mild weather reduces the demand for oil, reducing any rise in price resulting from cutbacks.

4 This will raise prices for futures dealing in rubber.

LIFFE options and financial futures

1 A futures contract is an agreement to buy or sell a fixed quantity of a commodity for delivery at a fixed date in the future at a price agreed in the present. An option is where the dealer takes out an option on a futures contract and will buy or sell only if it is profitable.

2 Speculators buy options because, although they might lose the initial purchase price of the option if they do not finalise the contract, they can make a large profit if the financial security rises sharply in price.

Interest rates

1 The Monetary Policy Committee.
2 They will set their rate above the MPC rate, according to the level of risk involved, but not so high as to lose out to competitors.
3 a) A Certificate of Deposit is issued by one bank to another which has deposited funds with it. It is an interest-bearing security.
   b) Treasury Bills are short-term bills sold by the Treasury to raise temporary funds for the government.
   c) Krugerrands are gold coins.

Exchange rates

1 An importer uses the Forex to buy or sell foreign currency for future delivery to cover itself against the potential rise or fall in the value of that currency.
2 'Bank buys' is the price at which banks will buy foreign currency from travellers. 'Bank sells' is the price at which the bank will sell that currency to travellers.

Glossary of terms

The following glossary gives definitions of terms and vocabulary not specifically defined in the text.

Accounting Standards Rules and regulations governing the measurement and/or disclosure of particular types of transactions.

Administration expenses Costs that are not associated with producing and delivering goods and services to the customer, e.g. marketing activities.

Alternative Investment Market (AIM) A market for smaller and newer companies on the Stock Exchange.

Balance sheet A snapshot of a firm's assets, liabilities and sources of capital at a moment in time.

Benchmark An appropriate measure of comparison, e.g. last year's wage bill would be a benchmark against which to measure this year's.

Blue chip companies Those with a long record of continuous and steadily rising profit and uninterrupted dividend payments.

Board of Directors Senior directors of a company who have been appointed to direct company activities.

Cadbury Committee A committee which devised a code (the Cadbury Code) aimed at tightening up various aspects of the financial supervision of companies whose recommendations included the setting up of remuneration and audit committees.

Chair of a company Individual in charge of the Board of Directors and the leading representative of shareholders.

Chief executive Leading representative of the manager and employees of a company, in charge of its day-to-day running.

Combined Code on Corporate Governance Bringing together the recommendations of the Cadbury, Greenbury and Hampel committees – the net effect of which has been to make company reporting more transparent, particularly in relation to directors' pay and perks, and the requirement for companies to comply with corporate governance requirements.

Companies House Name for the Companies Registry, where legally required information on public and private companies must be filed with the Registrar of Companies.

Company Any type of business that has a legal identity separate from its members; most companies are limited and most are registered under the Companies Act.

Cost of sales The cost of making the product and services sold to customers.

Directors People appointed by shareholders of a company to look after their interests.

Distribution costs The cost of getting the firm's product from the factory to the consumer.

Dividend Payment to shareholders out of company profits.

Loan stock Loans that can be bought and sold in the same way as shares in a company.

Nominal value The value at which a share is recorded in the accounting records.

Official List Main Stock Exchange market for established companies.

Ratio The relationship between one business variable and another, e.g. profit to sales.

Return on capital employed (ROCE) Profit before interest, expressed as a percentage of capital employed.

Settlement The date by which all purchases must be paid for by the buyer and delivered by the seller.

Share premium The difference between the amount received and the nominal value when a company issues new shares.

Solvency Ability to pay wages, supplier's bills and other obligations as they fall due.

Stakeholder Someone with an interest in the running of a business.

Tangible Physical items that you can touch and see.

Working capital The financial resources that enable a firm to operate on a day-to-day basis, e.g. having stock to sell, the ability to give customers credit and having cash to pay bills as they fall due.

Yield The rate of return to shareholders if their company's earnings were distributed to them as dividends; the higher the yield, the more money a shareholder earns.

Index